Annie Bell

gorgeouschristmas

Annie Bell

gorgeouschristmas

with photographs by Chris Alack

Kyle Cathie Ltd

First published in Great Britain in 2009 by
Kyle Cathie Limited
122 Arlington Road, London NW1 7HP
general.enquiries@kyle-cathie.com
www.kylecathie.com

978 1 85626 846 2

A CIP catalogue record for this title is available from the British Library.

10 9 8 7 6 5 4 3

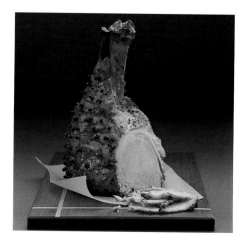

Editor: Suzanna de Jong
Design: pinkstripedesign@hotmail.com
Copy Editor: Annie Lee
Proofreader: Kay Halsey
Indexer: Alex Corrin
Photographer: Chris Alack
Home Economist: Kim Morphew
Prop Stylist: Sue Radcliffe
Production: Lisa Pinnell

Colour reproduction: Colourscan, Singapore
Printed and bound in Singapore by Star Standard Industries Pte Ltd

contents

introduction

Christmas is a time of pure magic. For those of us who take it seriously it is a season within a season, one we anticipate for weeks and sometimes months in advance. Where will we be, what will we be doing, who will we be celebrating with, and of course what will we be eating? The day itself, though, is only part of the season, and the run-up is just as much if not more fun, with all that planning and dreaming. The shopping, parties and celebrating hit a high note from the end of November. Even if we say we're not going to do anything about Christmas until December, for most of us this is a rule that lasts about as long as our New Year's resolution.

Visual charm is writ large in the cooking we aspire to at Christmas. I have a horror of 'tasteful' or 'designer' Christmases: trees, cards, cakes, you name it. Bring on the glitter and coloured fairy lights, the kitsch Christmas tree decorations, the ceramic Santa or nativity scene that kept you enraptured as a child, those rusting cookie cutters and vintage cake decorations. One of the joys of being that little bit older is that Christmas had yet to be invaded by commercial merchandising. I would rather travel back to an age of innocence, even if it does mean making paper chains on my own.

So retro it is. Our love of Christmas has everything to do with our childhood, trying to recreate what we left behind. And as soon as we have children that urge becomes compulsive. So pity those couples who grew up with very different traditions, trying to agree on what the order of the day should be. In our house, thankfully, that goes little further than, 'Should we have Christmas lunch [my way] or Christmas dinner [his way].'

The good news is how readily the food brings those memories flooding back. It doesn't have to be wildly ambitious, technically brilliant or even the finest money can buy. If your mum always served miniature sausage rolls with the drinks before the turkey, that's what will do it for you. Memory underwrites our sense of smell, so whenever we taste and draw in all those lovely Christmas scents, we travel back to happy childhood times. None of the recipes here seek to rewrite history. They are mainly based on my own traditional childhood

Christmases, with an eye to exploiting some more alluring modern trends like sherry and quince-glazed ham and bûche de Noël.

Christmas Eve was a time of hushed anticipation in our house, with children parked in front of a film while my mother tried to get ahead with the preparation for Christmas lunch and make sure the house was all set. The party proper would begin that evening. And then Christmas morning arrived, with glittery felt stockings groaning with treasure laid at the end of the bed. We all traipsed off to church, everyone in their Christmas best, then home for Champagne, presents under the tree, and a huge traditional lunch. This was played out year after year, the same pattern and the same food, most of which I now cook for my own family.

And I love revisiting these traditions: how can you be bored with turkey and Christmas pud when they only come round once a year? So the chapters that follow seek to cover all the favourites, and to cater for all the different occasions. Kicking off is Hand-Me-Rounds, nothing as fiddly as a canapé, but relaxed and yummy eats like miniature sausage rolls, smoked salmon blinis, toasted Stilton and pickled walnut sandwiches, and devils on horseback. Little Pots and Big Pies covers bijou potted savouries and pâtés for eating with toast and a bowl of soup, and hearty meaty pies you can make well in advance, great for a hungry horde.

Gorgeous Birds and All the Trimmings do what they say, and hopefully you will find every possible aside you could wish for, a special way with bread sauce, cranberry sauce, honey-mustard roast chipolatas, and lots of stuffings. And it doesn't have to be turkey – roast goose with prune and apple stuffing, roast duck with

black pudding, and partridge with crispy crumbs and bacon sing just as loudly. Finally there are all those lovely soups and toasties that follow with the leftovers.

On to the sweet chapters: Christmas is a time when you can go to town with lovely baked goodies and puds, and chocolates to make and give. The Christmas pudding recipe was handed down to me by my grandmother, and is a vintage classic, while white Christmas cheesecake is a new addition to the repertoire, as is the traditional French Twelfth Night cake, something to celebrate with around New Year.

If I am honest I do sometimes muse on an easy Christmas, and in that sense know I am my own worst enemy. It is the cook who sets the goalposts: whether to make stuffing or accept the butcher's offer to stuff the bird for you, whether to exploit the local pâtisserie and order a bûche de Noël or to set to it at home. The last thing I want anyone to feel is that they have to prepare absolutely everything from scratch. I hope I have covered everything you might want to make, but that doesn't mean you should be trying to make it all.

My family always tease me about my lists: I have lists for everything, and they grow in number and length the closer we get to Christmas. But it's advance planning that ensures you actually enjoy the festivities yourself. Any cooking you do in the days leading to the run-up will be time well invested. With carefully planned menus you'll spend minimum time in the kitchen during the days after Christmas, and gear up again for New Year's Eve. That said, the more helping hands the better; if the work's shared it won't seem like a burden. There are plenty of jobs that don't require any skill, like peeling spuds, grating cheese, or making a stock.

I try to balance things, and the easy route comes in the form of luxury. I intersperse things I've made myself with simple dishes of smoked salmon or eel, oysters and large prawns with mayonnaise, watercress and fine bread. Or a selection of lovely cheeses, a Vacherin Mont d'Or warmed beside the fire for a couple of hours, with air-dried ham, chicory leaves and walnuts. Parfaits and pâtés too will see you through meals and cocktail eats, spread on to blinis or toast, while puddings can take advantage of all those fruits in brandy, such as griottine cherries, spooned over ice cream, or can just be a couple of chocolate truffles. Think of Christmas dinner itself as a very big Sunday lunch, and it doesn't feel so daunting. All that's left is to enjoy it all. *Santé*.

the art of decoration

Part of the fun of making Christmas cakes and puds lies with decorating them. I tend to start collecting candy sticks, marshmallow snowmen and gold dragees while I'm out Christmas shopping. But there are plenty of on-line shops that remove the footwork. Try Lakeland (www.lakeland.co.uk); Jane Asher Party Cakes (www.jane-asher.co.uk); Supercook (www.supercook.co.uk); Squires Kitchen (www.squires-shop.com); and the Sugar Shack (www.sugarshack.co.uk).

bowls and racks

I always make my Christmas puddings in Mason Cash pudding basins, and mix them in an old-fashioned cane-weave mixing bowl. For stockists: sales@rayware.co.uk

When roasting a goose or duck, a rack will ensure that the fat runs off into the base of the roasting dish, allowing the bird to crisp and colour all over. Le Creuset (www.lecreuset.co.uk) produce two special racks that fit within their roasting dishes, with handles for ease of lifting the bird out at the end.

hand-me-rounds

The exhilarating pop of a Champagne cork and gentle hiss of foam brings with it the most vexing of the season's demands, cocktail eats. Thinking in miniature is the last thing we have time to do in between all that wrapping and last-minute shopping. To which there is one immediate solution. Banish all thoughts of anything fiddly that will go down in one bite, and plan for eats that are that little bit bigger.

Things on toast, small sausage rolls and generous mouthfuls of smoked salmon are altogether more relaxing and homely than miniature quiches and doll's house canapés. Their role, after all, is to take the edge off our hunger before dinner, but equally, if you keep them coming, with a big pile of warm mince pies towards the end, they will also replace dinner. So it can be a lovely way of entertaining lots of friends and family without all the work that goes into preparing a proper meal.

Old-fashioned savouries get wolfed down, and make hearty no-nonsense appetisers. They are spiced with distinctly British notes like mace and Worcestershire sauce, mustard and capers. The most famous are rarebits, angels and devils on horseback, and anchovies with scrambled eggs, known as a Scotch woodcock. Devilled chicken livers and kidneys are also popular, and I have a soft spot for herring roes.

The buttery scent of pastry emerging from the oven as you walk through the door makes the best possible welcome. I marvel at puff pastry and the way it rises within minutes to exquisite gossamer-fine layers. Crisp straws and little biscuits make a star turn at any drinks party, and their delicacy and prettiness belie the speed and ease of preparation. To their credit, such pastries can also be prepared several days in advance and reheated for a few minutes before serving.

Few can resist a homemade cheese straw – I certainly can't. The best ones taste like that crispy bit of toasted cheese on the bottom of the grill pan after you've cooked a rarebit. I find a mixture of Gruyère and Parmesan gives a good balance of flavour and crunch.

cheese straws

225g puff pastry
25g freshly grated Parmesan
25g grated Gruyère
a knife tip of cayenne pepper
1 egg yolk, blended with
  1 tablespoon milk
groundnut or vegetable oil

Serves 8
Makes 20–25

Preheat the oven to 180°C fan/200°C/gas mark 6. Thinly roll out the pastry, to about 1mm, on a lightly floured surface into a large rectangle about 30 x 50cm wide. Place the long sides facing you, and trim them. Combine the Parmesan and Gruyère with the cayenne pepper in a bowl and scatter over the top half of pastry, leaving a 1cm edge. Brush this with the eggwash and bring the lower edge up over it. Roll the sheet to seal the edges and compress the cheese – you should have a strip about 15cm wide. Cut this into 1cm straws.

Holding one end in either hand, twist each strip to give you about 5 turns, and lay them 2cm apart on one or two oiled baking sheets, pressing the edges well down to ensure they don't unravel as they cook. Bake for 12–15 minutes, until they are evenly golden, turning the trays round halfway through. The bottom tray may take a few minutes longer than the top.

Loosen the straws with a palette knife (any that break are cook's tips), and ideally serve while still warm, or newly cooled. I like to stack them in glasses, but alternatively you can arrange them in a bowl or on a plate. They can also be stored for several days in an airtight container, and reheated for 5 minutes in an oven preheated to 150°C fan/170°C/gas mark 3.

We are so used to the convenience of ready-roasted nuts that we have all but forgotten what a treat they are freshly roasted and salted, when they have that wonderful squeaky-clean bite. You also get to combine all your favourites for a tailor-made mix. I have a particular fondness for roast almonds, cashews and macadamias, with dried cherries for festive cheer.

christmas fruit and nuts

2 teaspoons unsalted butter, softened

100g cashews

150g almonds, skinned

100g macadamias

3 tablespoons coarse sea salt

cayenne pepper

75g dried cherries or cranberries

Serves 8
Makes approx. 425g

Preheat the oven to 140°C fan/160°C/gas mark 2½. Grease a baking tray with the butter and spread the cashews and almonds in a single layer on top. Bake for 10 minutes, then scatter over the macadamias. Bake for another 35 minutes, by which time they should be a pale creamy gold.

Scatter the sea salt over a sheet of baking paper. Tip the nuts on top and use a teaspoon to toss and rub the salt through them. Wrap the paper up into a package and set aside overnight (the minimum they need is 1 hour if you are doing them at the last minute). On unwrapping the nuts, dust them with a generous knife tip of cayenne pepper and shake off the excess salt. Transfer to a bowl and mix in the dried cherries or cranberries.

This three-in-one looks as though you've gone to a great deal of trouble, when in truth it's just one recipe, with the dough flavoured in three different ways. They're deliciously short and buttery, and way, way better than anything you are likely to be able to buy.

cocktail shortbreads

Dough

150g plain flour
75g ground almonds
150g salted butter (e.g. Brittany
    butter), chilled and diced

Flavourings

1 heaped teaspoon poppy seeds,
    plus extra for rolling
finely grated zest of 1 lemon
1 heaped teaspoon sesame seeds,
    plus extra for rolling
½ teaspoon ground cumin
25g freshly grated Parmesan
cayenne pepper
vegetable oil

Serves 10

Place the flour, ground almonds and butter in the bowl of a food processor and briefly whiz to fine crumbs – it's important to heed the 'briefly' here.

Divide the mixture between three bowls. Stir the poppy seeds and lemon zest into one, the sesame seeds and cumin into the other, and the Parmesan and a suspicion of cayenne pepper into the third bowl. Bring each mixture together into a ball, using your hands. Form the cheese dough into a roughly shaped sausage about 3cm in diameter, wrap it in clingfilm and give it a roll to smooth it out. Wrap the remaining two balls of dough in clingfilm. You can freeze them at this point, otherwise chill them all for an hour or two.

Preheat the oven to 140°C fan/160°C/gas mark 2½, and brush a couple of baking sheets with oil. Knead the poppy seed dough until it is pliable, then roll pieces into balls a little smaller than a cherry, roll them in poppy seeds in a small bowl, and place slightly apart on a baking sheet. Repeat this with the sesame seed dough, this time rolling them into a slightly elongated shape and coating them in sesame seeds, then slice the roll of cheese dough about 1cm thick. Bake the biscuits for 35–40 minutes, until the cheese ones are lightly golden, by which time the others will also be cooked inside. Loosen the cheese biscuits with a palette knife, and leave them all to cool. They will keep well for up to a week in an airtight container.

Like cocktail sausages, a plate of these handed round comes back empty within minutes. Delicious served warm from the oven, you can also make them in advance. If you can find puff pastry made with butter, so much the better. And as ever, your best bet with sausage meat is a banger with a good pedigree – simply slip off their skins.

miniature sausage rolls

250g puff pastry
250g sausage meat
1 teaspoon Dijon mustard
1 teaspoon wholegrain mustard
1 egg yolk, whisked with
   1 tablespoon milk

Serves 6

Preheat the oven to 180°C fan/200°C/gas mark 6. Thinly roll out the pastry on a lightly floured surface into a rectangle the width of a sheet of A4 paper. Trim the long edges and cut this into two finger-long strips, about 8cm wide. Using your hands, divide the sausage meat between the strips, rolling it into a long thin cylinder a little fatter than a chipolata, and laying it down the length of the pastry. Blend the mustards together and use a knife to smear this mixture in a line down the length of sausage meat.

Paint one long edge of each piece of pastry with a 1cm rim of eggwash. Fold the unpainted edge over the sausage meat, and then the painted edge on top and press together. Trim the ends of excess pastry, and if necessary cut the sausage rolls in half to fit a baking tray, but otherwise lay the two rolls on a baking sheet, sealed side down. Score the top of the sausage rolls with diagonal slits 1cm apart, and paint the top and sides with eggwash. Bake for 25–30 minutes.

Leave to cool for 15 minutes, then cut diagonally into 1–3cm slices and serve warm as an appetiser. They can also be rewarmed for 10 minutes in an oven preheated to 150°C fan/170°C/gas mark 3.

Elegant little cocktail biscuits, like those Roka Crispies that have so long featured at all the best cocktail parties. I find it easiest to roll out a length of ready-rolled puff pastry, which is the right width, rather than a piece from a block. You can make up the roll and keep it in the fridge for several days, ready to slice and bake.

catherine wheels

approx. 15 saffron filaments
6 salted anchovy fillets, finely chopped
40g unsalted butter, softened
100g puff pastry, i.e. ¼ of a 375g
   ready-rolled pack

Serves 6–8
Makes approx. 25

Grind the saffron filaments in a pestle and mortar, then add the chopped anchovies and work to a paste. Add the butter and blend.

Assuming you are using a quarter of a pack of ready-rolled pastry, roll this into a rectangle about 25 x 30cm on a lightly floured work surface and trim the ends. Spread the butter over the surface and roll the pastry back up again into a long thin tube about 2cm in diameter. Wrap in clingfilm and chill for a couple of hours or overnight.

Carefully slice the roll into rounds just under a centimetre thick, ideally using a small serrated knife to avoid squashing them, discarding the ends. Lay these out on a baking sheet spaced slightly apart, weight them down with another baking sheet, and bake for 12–15 minutes. Serve warm or at room temperature. They can also be rewarmed for 5 minutes in an oven preheated to 180°C fan/200°C/gas mark 6.

Little toasted sandwiches are exactly what you feel like come the second glass of Champagne, when dinner still seems some way off. Just enough to warm you and take the edge off your hunger without ruining your appetite altogether. The sweetness of pickled walnuts makes them an ideal relish for Stilton, and you just may have a nice truckle standing by.

toasted stilton and pickled walnut sandwiches

unsalted butter, softened

4 slices of granary or other nutty brown bread

80g Stilton (weight excluding rind), sliced

3 pickled walnuts, sliced

a few slivers of red onion

sprigs of watercress to garnish

Serves 4

Butter the bread on both sides. Cover two of the slices with a layer of Stilton, then add the pickled walnuts and onion. Close the sandwiches with the top layer of bread and press down. They can be prepared to this point in advance.

If you have a sandwich toaster, you can cook them in this. Otherwise, heat a large frying pan (ideally non-stick) over a high heat for several minutes, or two pans if one can't hold both sandwiches at once. Place the sandwiches in the pan, turn the heat down to medium low and cook for 3–5 minutes each side, until golden on the outside and oozing melted cheese. Using a sharp knife, cut the crusts off the toasted sandwiches and slice each one into four triangles. Serve with a few sprigs of watercress.

These need no introduction: crisp rolls of bacon encasing a jammy prune soaked in tea and port. I find I get more evenly gold and crisp devils by roasting them in a hot oven rather than fussing over a grill pan.

devils on horseback

12 ready-to-eat stoned prunes
2 tablespoons port
4 tablespoons tea
12 rashers of rindless unsmoked streaky bacon
1 tablespoon honey mustard*

Serves 4–6
Makes 12

Submerge the prunes in the port and tea in a small bowl, and leave to soak overnight.

Preheat the oven to 220°C fan/240°C/gas mark 9. Drain off any residual liquid from the prunes, and lay the bacon rashers out on a board. Brush a little mustard down the length of each rasher and roll it around a prune. Place the rolls spaced slightly apart in a roasting dish, and roast for 12 minutes until golden and crisp, turning them halfway through and using a palette knife to loosen them. Leave to stand for 5–10 minutes, then skewer a cocktail stick through the bacon and serve.

*Colman's Honey Mustard is ideal here, but failing that blend 2 teaspoons of prepared English mustard with 1 teaspoon of set honey.

I didn't try herring roes until I was well into my twenties, in a West Country pub having supper with my father. They were dished up on well-buttered crisp brown toast with a squeeze of lemon and lots of chopped parsley, and I've been a fan ever since. They're hugely underrated, an affordable delicacy and widely available.

herring roes on toast

50g unsalted butter, plus extra
    for the toast
225g herring roes
50g plain flour, seasoned with
    sea salt and black pepper
4 slices of unsweetened brioche or
    white bread
1 tablespoon capers, rinsed
1 tablespoon chopped fresh
    flat-leaf parsley
4 lemon wedges to serve

Serves 4

Melt the 50g butter in a small saucepan over a gentle heat, skim off the surface foam, decant the clear liquid and discard the milky residue at the bottom. You will need to fry the roes in two batches. Heat half the clarified butter in a large frying pan over a medium-high heat, dust the roes in the seasoned flour and cook for 1–2 minutes each side, until lightly coloured. Remove to a plate and cook the remainder in the same fashion.

While cooking the roes, toast and butter the brioche or bread. Cut the crusts off each slice and halve into soldiers. Divide the roes between them, scatter over the capers and parsley and serve with the lemon wedges.

I suppose anything threaded on to a cocktail stick might be seen as fiddly, but they do lie at the utilitarian end of dainty, and slip down very well. As light as a morsel of sushi, and so good with Champagne.

smoked salmon and prawn skewers

150g smoked salmon, cut into
   broad strips, approx. 8 x 3–4cm
approx. 18 cooked and peeled
   king prawns (80g)
a squeeze of lemon juice
black pepper
finely chopped fresh chives or
   flat-leaf parsley

Serves 6–8
Makes approx. 18

Roll up each strip of smoked salmon and skewer it with a cocktail stick, then pop a prawn on to the end curved side first. Arrange these on a plate. Cover and chill until required. To serve, squeeze over a little lemon juice, grind over some black pepper and scatter with chives or parsley.

These are my great standby for impromptu drinks parties; they're so easy and they always go down well. To which end I make sure I always have a packet or two of blinis, some smoked salmon and keta roe in the fridge over Christmas.

You could also serve the smoked salmon on small plates with a fork to eat on laps or standing around. In this case double the amount of smoked salmon, halve each slice into two long strips about 5cm wide, and arrange on one or two plates. Just before eating squeeze a little lemon juice over the salmon and season with black pepper. Accompany with the keta roe and warm blinis for everyone to help themselves.

blinis with smoked salmon

100g fromage frais
100g jar of salmon keta roe
175g sliced smoked salmon,
    brown meat cut out
approx. 24 cocktail blinis
½ lemon
black pepper

Serves 6–8
Makes approx. 24

Spoon the fromage frais into a bowl and gently fold in the keta roe. Transfer to a small clean bowl. Cut the smoked salmon into approx. 5cm morsels. If making these in advance, cover the keta roe and salmon with clingfilm and reserve in a cool place or chill. Bring back to room temperature 30 minutes before serving.

To serve, preheat the oven to 180°C fan/200°C/gas mark 6. Lay the blinis out on one or two baking sheets and warm through for 2–3 minutes. Splodge ½ teaspoon or so of the keta roe on to each blini, fold a piece of salmon on top, squeeze over a little lemon and grind over some black pepper.

party drinks

mulled rosé

1 bottle of rosé
150ml Cointreau
3 star anise
10 cloves
3 thin slices of clementine or satsuma
1 x 7cm cinnamon stick
2 tablespoons fresh inner rose petals or 1 tablespoon dried rosebuds

Serves 6

Place all the ingredients except for the rose petals or buds in a small saucepan and gently heat, without allowing the wine to boil. Leave to infuse for a few minutes, then scatter over the rose petals or buds and ladle into small cups or glasses, first popping in a metal teaspoon to stop them cracking. You could also transfer the mulled wine to a glass bowl to serve, but again protect it first with a metal spoon.

kir normande

2 tablespoons cassis
1 bottle of dry cider, chilled

Serves 6

Spoon a teaspoon of cassis into six wineglasses and top up with very cold dry cider.

seville cocktails

300ml sweet sherry (e.g. Harveys Bristol Cream)
75ml vodka
150ml fresh orange juice
ice cubes
slivers of orange and a few coffee beans

Serves 6

Stir the sherry, vodka and orange juice in a jug with ice, some slivers of orange and a few coffee beans. Stir and serve.

ginger nectar

325ml ginger wine
200ml amaretto
2 tablespoons brandy
325ml still mineral water
2 knobs of ginger in syrup, thinly sliced
3 thin slices of lemon, halved into half moons
ice cubes

Serves 6

You can chill the bottles before mixing the cocktails, but it's not essential. Combine the ginger wine, amaretto, brandy and mineral water in a jug and stir to blend, then add the sliced ginger and lemon. Add lots of ice cubes, stir and serve.

cranberry bellinis

200g cranberries
50g caster sugar
150ml fresh orange or clementine juice
1 bottle of chilled Champagne or prosecco

Serves 6

Place the cranberries, sugar and orange or clementine juice in a small saucepan and bring to the boil. Cover the pan and simmer over a low heat for 5 minutes until soft, then press through a fine-mesh sieve and leave to cool. You should have about 200ml of thin purée. Cover and chill.

Give the purée a stir, then spoon a rounded tablespoon into six glasses, fill up with fizz and give it a quick twizzle to blend.

little pots
and big pies

Little potted savouries and big hearty pies have endless appeal. It must have something to do with how they are served – food that is neatly contained is particularly comforting. And all these dishes can be made in advance, so they perfectly balance out Christmas dinner, which with all the planning in the world is a last-minute juggling act, best performed on one too few glasses of Champagne. Whereas here you can separate out the work from the event.

The chicken liver parfait is a classic, and as close as you can get to foie gras without guilt. Its main sin is the amount of butter, which accounts for its luxurious melt-in-the mouth feel. Along with the potted smoked salmon, this is another of my last-minute drinks stand-bys, spread on little pieces of toast with a smidgen of chutney. And with all those soups to come once you've finished up the turkey, it completes supper, with generous slabs of toasted sourdough or wholegrain bread and a pile of plump, peppery watercress. But for those who want to go the extra mile of a 'proper' pâté, the duck and pistachio terrine is that tad more formal, but without demanding that you make best friends with the butcher in advance to acquire the necessary elusive cuts of meat that are a terrine-maker's staple.

Beef pies are always a hit with family and friends, but the real favourite in our house is a retro turkey and ham number, a good old-fashioned potato-topped pie that makes the most of all the leftovers. And Christmas and New Year's Eve are the perfect times to be eating a fish pie, as you're bound to be hitting the shops in the day or so beforehand, so you can relish eating it really fresh and then settle to more meaty fare in the days to come. This boulangère pie rings the changes with a top of finely sliced potatoes, in lieu of mash, that turn deliciously crispy at the edges.

Glamorous potted savouries that can be knocked up in a jiffy are endlessly useful. One advantage to making your own is being able to pack them into a pretty dish or little jars. They make great presents, especially if you're going round to friends for dinner. While if you're at home, you have an instant hand-me-round piled on to blinis with drinks, or a light supper with thin crisp toast and a little salad. Some lightly cooked quail's eggs or a poached egg would be delicious with the buttery salmon too.

potted hot-smoked salmon

200g unsalted butter
600g hot-smoked salmon,
    skinned and flaked
Tabasco
30g (2 tablespoons) small capers,
    plus a few extra to decorate

2 teaspoons finely chopped fresh
    tarragon, plus a few sprigs or
    leaves to decorate
1 tablespoon finely chopped fresh
    flat-leaf parsley
juice of ½ lemon

Serves 6

Melt half the butter in a large frying pan, add the fish and stir to coat. Season with a few splashes of Tabasco, and stir in the capers, herbs and lemon juice. Press the mixture into a bowl, about 1 litre in volume, or into small ramekins. Cover with clingfilm and chill for an hour until it has begun to set.

Drape a few sprigs or leaves of tarragon over the surface, scatter over a few more capers, then melt the remaining butter and pour this over, submerging the herbs. Cover the dish and chill for several hours or overnight.

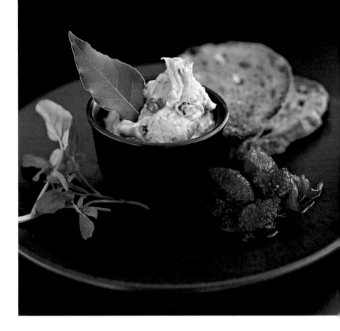

If you have to choose just one pâté to have on hand over Christmas, this supremely simple buttery parfait will see you through. And as with other pâtés, a green salad, some toasted sourdough and a jar of chutney alongside and you have supper fit for a king.

chicken liver parfait

225g unsalted butter

225g chicken livers, fatty
  membranes removed

1 bay leaf

2 sprigs of fresh thyme

sea salt, black pepper

1 shallot, peeled and finely chopped

1 garlic clove, peeled and
  finely chopped

2 tablespoons sweet wine or sherry

2 tablespoons Armagnac or brandy

1 tablespoon crème fraîche

freshly grated nutmeg

1 x 15g jar of summer truffles,
  finely chopped (optional)

bay leaves and green or pink
  peppercorns to decorate

Serves 6

Melt 25g of the butter in a large frying pan over a medium heat. When the foam starts to subside, add the chicken livers and the herbs, season and fry for 3 minutes, until they are golden on the outside but still pink in the centre, turning the livers halfway through. Discard the herbs and tip the livers with any juices into a blender.

Add another knob of butter to the pan and cook the shallot and garlic gently for a couple of minutes until glossy and translucent. Add the sweet wine or sherry and the brandy to the pan and simmer until the liquid has all but disappeared. Tip the contents of the frying pan into the blender, add the crème fraîche and purée. Leave to cool for about 20 minutes.

Dice the remaining butter, add to the blender, and blend until the parfait is really smooth and creamy. Add a grinding of nutmeg and adjust the seasoning. I like to pass the parfait through a fine sieve to ensure it's as silky as possible, but you don't have to. Stir in the truffle if including. Spoon the pâté into a bowl, smooth the surface, and decorate with bay leaves and peppercorns. Cover and either freeze or chill. It keeps well for several days in the fridge. Leave it for 20 minutes out of the fridge for it to soften before serving.

This derives from our local gastropub in London, the Havelock, where they make a mean terrine. Don't be put off by all the draining – it's important to extract the liquid so that the terrine holds together. This is good dished up with a leafy salad.

duck and pistachio terrine

4–6 slices of air-dried ham,
   e.g. Parma or San Daniele
6–8 duck breasts (approx. 1.3kg)
150g crème fraîche
3 medium egg yolks
sea salt
1 tablespoon green peppercorns,
   rinsed and finely chopped
1 tablespoon fresh tarragon leaves
50g shelled roasted pistachios
chutney and toasted sourdough
   to serve

Serves 6

Heat the oven to 140°C fan/160°C/gas mark 2½. Arrange the slices of ham widthways in a 22cm/1.2 litre loaf tin so they overlap, draping the ends up the sides. Placing the duck breasts fat side down on the chopping board, finely slice across the breast to give three or four fine escalopes, reserving the fat if wished*.

Whisk the crème fraîche and egg yolks in a large bowl, season with salt and stir in the peppercorns. Add the duck slices about a third at a time to the bowl, lightly seasoning them with salt first, and toss to coat with the mixture. Lay the duck slices in the terrine, scattering over the tarragon leaves and pistachios as you go. Fold any overhanging ham over the top, then cover the terrine with foil. Place the tin in a roasting dish, with boiling water to come three-quarters of the way up the sides, and bake for 1 hour. Drain off the juices that have collected around the terrine, leave it to cool covered with foil and then drain it again. Cut out a piece of card to fit the top, weight it with a couple of cans or jars and chill overnight.

If any more liquid has collected, drain this off, run a knife around the terrine and turn it out on to a plate or board. Using kitchen paper, gently wipe the surface of the ham to tidy it up. Cut into thick slices using a sharp knife, and accompany with chutney and toasted sourdough.

*With all those potatoes to roast over Christmas you can make good use of the duck fat. Slice and gently heat it in an oven preheated to 140°C fan/160°C/gas mark 2½ for 30 minutes. Strain the rendered fat into a bowl, leave to cool, then cover and chill.

No one is expecting you to whiz up little soufflés as the gateway to dinner or to alleviate a light appetite, so how timely to be able to whip them out of the freezer straight into the oven for a little instant luxury. A great one for any lone vegetarians present who might otherwise miss out with all the meaty fare on offer.

mushroom soufflés

Moulds

70g unsalted butter
30g freshly grated Parmesan

Soufflé

200g chestnut or wild mushrooms,
   picked over and trimmed
60g unsalted butter
sea salt, black pepper
30g plain flour
200ml full-cream milk
3 tablespoons freshly grated Parmesan
freshly grated nutmeg
3 medium egg yolks
5 medium egg whites

Serves 6

To prepare the moulds, clarify the butter by melting it in a small saucepan. Skim off the white foam on the surface and pour off the clear yellow liquid, leaving behind the milky residue in the base. Swill the inside of six 150ml ramekins with the clarified butter and dust them with the Parmesan. Chill the dishes until this firms up.

To make the soufflé, finely chop the mushrooms in a food processor. Melt half the butter in a large frying pan over a medium heat, add the mushrooms, season and fry for 6–9 minutes, until the mixture appears dry and the pieces of mushroom are separating out. Melt the remaining butter in a small non-stick saucepan, stir in the flour and cook the roux for a couple of minutes. Take off the heat and very gradually incorporate the milk, then bring the sauce to the boil and simmer over a low heat for 4 minutes, stirring frequently. Remove the pan from the heat, stir in 2 tablespoons of Parmesan and the mushrooms, and season with salt, pepper and nutmeg. Allow to cool for a few minutes, then beat in the egg yolks and transfer to a large bowl.

Preheat the oven to 190°C fan/210°C/gas mark 6. Whisk the egg whites in another large bowl until stiff. Fold a couple of spoons of the whisked egg white into the sauce to lighten it and then fold in the remainder in two goes. Pour the soufflé mixture into the dishes and scatter the rest of the Parmesan evenly over the surface. The soufflés can be frozen at this point, in which case cover and pop them into the freezer without delay. Otherwise place them on a baking tray, place it immediately in the oven and cook for about 9–11 minutes. Avoid opening the door; the soufflés should ideally be baveuse or slightly wet in the centre. If cooking them from frozen allow 17–20 minutes.

These miniature pies offer up the best bits of steak and kidney and cottage pie rolled into one, nuggets of meat and lots of lovely rich brown gravy bubbling up at the sides of a buttery mash.

beef, chestnut and brandy pies

Beef

50–75g unsalted butter

1.2kg chuck steak, trimmed of fat
  and diced

150g unsmoked lardons, or rashers
  of rindless unsmoked streaky
  bacon, diced

2 onions, peeled, halved and thinly sliced

3 garlic cloves, peeled and
  finely chopped

90ml brandy

1 tablespoon plain flour

225ml red wine

225ml beef stock or water

1 bay leaf

1 small bunch of fresh thyme,
  tied with string

sea salt, black pepper

200g cooked and peeled chestnuts,
  quartered

2 tablespoons mushroom ketchup
  (optional)

On Top

1.5kg maincrop potatoes, peeled and
  halved or quartered if large

700g parsnips, peeled and cut
  into pieces

150g unsalted butter, diced

Serves 6

Heat 50g of butter in a large cast-iron casserole over a medium-high heat. Add some of the cubed meat, leaving plenty of space between the pieces, and sear on all sides (without seasoning), then remove and cook the remainder in the same fashion, adding more butter if necessary. Add the lardons to the pan and fry for several minutes until lightly coloured, stirring occasionally, then add the onion and continue to fry for 5–7 minutes, until really golden, stirring now and again. Add the garlic just before the end.

Return the meat to the pan and give everything a stir, then flambé with the brandy. I find it easiest to heat a little at a time in a ladle over a gas flame, swirling it around until it ignites, and then gradually pour it over. Once the flames have died down stir in the flour, then add the wine and stock or water, the herbs and a little seasoning (bearing in mind that the lardons will do a lot of the work). Bring to the boil, then cover and cook over a very low heat for 1–1½ hours, or until the meat is tender and sitting in a rich golden gravy. Stir occasionally, especially towards the end, to prevent it from catching on the bottom. Discard the herbs and stir in the chestnuts and mushroom ketchup if using, then transfer to a bowl, cover and leave to cool.

Bring a large pan of salted water to the boil, add the potatoes and parsnips, bring back to a simmer and cook until tender. Drain them and leave for a minute or two to steam dry, then pass through a mouli-légumes or a sieve back into the pan. Add the butter, and seasoning to taste. Divide the pie filling between six 500ml ovenproof dishes, and smooth the mash on top. Using the end of a teaspoon, make indentations in the potato, then leave to cool. The pies can be frozen at this point, otherwise cover and chill until required. Cook them (defrosted) for 40–45 minutes in an oven preheated to 180°C fan/200°C/gas mark 6 until the pies are golden on top, and the gravy is bubbling at the sides.

The treat here is the crisp slivers of bread on top of the casserole, which are slightly soggy where they've soaked up the gravy underneath. The lengthy list of ingredients that go to making special-occasion casseroles belies their ease of making. Like any other, this is all tied up within a twenty-minute flurry at the start of cooking. Look out for Chantenay carrots; a fat baby carrot, they're perfect casserole material.

venison carbonade

50g unsalted butter, plus extra for spreading

3 onions, peeled, halved and sliced

2 garlic cloves, peeled and smashed

900g stewing venison, diced

2 tablespoons plain flour

sea salt, black pepper

300ml Guinness

600ml beef stock

200g small carrots, peeled

2 sticks of celery, trimmed and sliced

about 10 sprigs of fresh thyme,
   tied into a bunch

2 bay leaves

2 teaspoons light brown sugar

1 teaspoon red wine vinegar

approx. 20 thin slices of French bread
   (about ½ baguette)

Dijon mustard

Serves 4–6

Preheat the oven to 160°C fan/180°C/gas mark 4. Melt half the butter in a large cast-iron casserole over a medium heat, add the onions and fry for 8–10 minutes until golden, stirring occasionally, adding the garlic just before the end, then remove them to a bowl. Toss the venison with the flour and some seasoning in a bowl, and seal it in two batches, adding half the remaining butter with each one. You may need to turn the heat up towards the end.

Return the onions to the casserole, pour over the Guinness and beef stock, and add the carrots, celery, herbs, sugar, vinegar and some seasoning. Bring the liquid to the boil, then cover and cook in the oven for 1½ hours.

Remove the casserole from the oven and turn the temperature up to 180°C fan/200°C/gas mark 6. Season the stew to taste. Butter the slices of French bread on one side, and spread with mustard on the other. Arrange these so they overlap, mustard side down, in rows on top of the casserole, and return it to the oven for another 30–40 minutes, until they are golden and crisp. Serve straight away. If making the casserole in advance, reheat it on the stove top, and finish with the bread slices just before serving.

A homemade steak and kidney pie makes a special dinner, and I often make up the filling and the pastry in advance and freeze them. It's a great one for New Year's Eve, as well as for day two or three of the festivities when you still have a full house but the enthusiasm for cooking yet another meal may be waning. Dish it up with a big bowl of mash (the Christmas champ would be divine), and a down-to-earth veggie such as cabbage that will keep it in the right rustic vein.

steak and guinness pie with wild mushrooms

5 tablespoons vegetable oil

2 leeks, trimmed and sliced

1 celery heart, sliced

1kg chuck steak, trimmed
    of fat and diced

2 heaped tablespoons plain flour

100ml medium sherry

200ml Guinness or other stout

200ml beef stock

1 bay leaf

3 sprigs of fresh thyme

sea salt, black pepper

250g lambs' kidneys, fat and ducts
    removed, sliced

300g wild mushrooms, e.g. girolles or
    porcini, or flavoursome cultivated
    ones, picked over and sliced

600g shortcrust pastry

1 egg yolk, mixed with 1 tablespoon
    milk

Serves 6

Heat 2 tablespoons of the oil in a large saucepan. Add the leeks and celery and cook gently over a low heat for about 8 minutes, until soft and just beginning to colour, stirring occasionally, then remove to a bowl. You will need to sear the meat in two goes. Turn the heat up, add half the meat to the pan and toss to seal and colour it, then remove it and cook the remainder. It's worth taking your time doing this, to ensure the meat colours properly, as this will help flavour the gravy. Return the meat and vegetables to the pan, sprinkle over the flour and stir to coat everything thoroughly. Pour over the sherry, Guinness and beef stock, stirring well into a smooth sauce, and add the herbs and some seasoning. Bring the liquid to a simmer, cover and braise over a low heat for 1–1½ hours or until the meat is tender, stirring occasionally, especially towards the end.

While it's cooking heat a tablespoon of oil in a frying pan over a high heat, add the kidneys, toss to seal them and then remove from the pan. Heat another tablespoon of oil, add half the mushrooms, and cook, tossing them, until they are soft and starting to colour. Add them to the kidneys and cook the remainder in the same way. Once the meat is cooked, remove the herbs and check the seasoning, stir in the mushrooms and kidneys and leave to cool. You can now freeze the filling, or use it fresh.

Preheat the oven to 190°C fan/210°C/gas mark 6. Thinly roll out two-thirds of the pastry on a floured work surface and line a deep 2–2.8 litre pie dish. Don't worry if you have to mend the pastry in places, it won't show once it's cooked. Tip the filling into the pie and paint the rim above it with eggwash. Thinly roll the remaining third of the pastry to fit the surface. Lay the pastry for the lid on top of the pie and trim the edges, leaving 1cm for shrinkage. Now press the edges together using a fork. Paint the surface with the eggwash. Roll out some of the pastry trimmings and cut out some stars to decorate the pie. Paint them with the eggwash, bake the pie for 45–50 minutes until nice and golden, and serve straight away.

My family are all retro diehards. I can spend hours dreaming up imaginative uses for leftover turkey and ham, only to arrive back at this pie – slivers of meat in a rich creamy white sauce made with the turkey stock, with a buttery mash on top. To the side? Well, frozen petits pois of course. And the real joy is that you can prepare it lock, stock and barrel well in advance and pop it into the oven forty minutes before you want to eat.

retro turkey and ham pie

Filling

60g unsalted butter

50g plain flour

100ml dry white wine

250ml turkey stock

150g crème fraîche

1 heaped teaspoon Dijon mustard

sea salt, black pepper

1 tablespoon groundnut or vegetable oil

250g chestnut or wild mushrooms,
   picked over and sliced if necessary

600g shredded leftover turkey

100g diced ham

2 tablespoons fresh tarragon leaves

Mash

1.5kg maincrop potatoes, peeled
   and halved if large

100g crème fraîche

50g unsalted butter

2 large egg yolks

Serves 6

To make the sauce, melt the butter in a medium-size non-stick saucepan, add the flour and allow the roux to seethe for a minute. Very gradually work in the wine, the turkey stock, then the crème fraîche, mustard and a little seasoning. Bring to the boil, stirring constantly, and simmer over a very low heat for 10 minutes, stirring occasionally. If any butter separates out simply stir vigorously until it is reincorporated.

At the same time heat the oil in a large frying pan, add the mushrooms, season and fry, cooking off any liquid that is given out until they are lightly coloured.

Taste the sauce to check the seasoning, then fold in the turkey, ham, mushrooms and tarragon leaves. Transfer the mixture to a 35cm oval gratin dish or other ovenproof dish with a 2.5 litre capacity that affords a large crispy surface. Leave to cool before you smooth the potato on top.

Bring a large pan of salted water to the boil and cook the potatoes until they are tender. Drain them into a sieve or colander and leave the surface moisture to evaporate for a minute or two. Pass through a mouli-légumes or a sieve back into the pan. Heat the crème fraîche with the butter and some seasoning and beat this into the mash, followed by the egg yolks. Smooth the mash over the top of the turkey, forking the surface into furrows.

Preheat the oven to 180°C fan/200°C/gas mark 6 and bake the pie for 40 minutes, until crusty and golden on top. You can cover and chill the pie until required, for up to 48 hours. In this case it may need a little longer in the oven.

Here a crispy layer of thinly sliced potatoes takes the place of the usual mash,
with haddock in parsley sauce below.

boulangère fish pie

900g haddock fillets (skin on)
300ml full-cream milk
sea salt, black pepper
60g unsalted butter
50g plain flour
100ml white wine
150ml double cream
1 heaped teaspoon Dijon mustard
6 salted anchovy fillets, sliced
8 tablespoons finely chopped
    fresh flat-leaf parsley
300g cooked and peeled king prawns
900g maincrop potatoes, peeled
2 tablespoons groundnut or
    vegetable oil

Serves 6

Place the haddock fillets skin side down in a large saucepan, cutting them to fit. Pour over the milk, season with black pepper and bring to the boil. Cover with a lid, leaving a gap for the steam to escape, and cook on a low heat for 4 minutes. Strain the cooking liquor into a bowl, and, once the fish is cool enough to handle, flake it as coarsely as possible, discarding the skin. If any additional liquid is given out beyond this point throw it away.

To make the béchamel, melt the butter in a medium-size non-stick saucepan, add the flour and allow the roux to seethe for a minute. Very gradually work in the wine, the fish cooking liquor and the cream, then stir in the mustard and the anchovies. Bring to the boil, stirring constantly, and simmer over a very low heat for 10 minutes, stirring occasionally. If any butter separates out simply stir vigorously until it is reincorporated. Taste to check the seasoning, then stir in the parsley and fold in the haddock and prawns. Transfer the fish to a 35cm oval gratin dish or other ovenproof dish with a 2.5 litre capacity that affords a large surface. Cover the surface with clingfilm and leave the fish to cool, which will help prevent the potatoes from sinking in. You can prepare the pie to this point several hours in advance, or the day beforehand if you are confident about the freshness of your fish, in which case chill it.

Preheat the oven to 190°C fan/210°C/gas mark 6. Slice the potatoes as finely as possible using a sharp knife, discarding the ends. Toss the potato slices in a large bowl with the oil and some seasoning and arrange them on top of the fish, overlapping like roof tiles, but quite tightly as you only want one layer. If using an oval gratin dish, start at the outside and then work inwards to the centre. Gently press down with your hands to level them. Bake the pie for about 40 minutes until the potatoes are crisp and golden at the edges, and tender.

An oldie but a goodie, based on Jane Grigson's famed 'salmon in pastry', which in turn was based on a dish served many years ago at the Hole in the Wall in Bath. It's one of those strange but magical combinations that has the air of being special every time you try it. If it's a 'blow the cholesterol' occasion, you could make a sleek little sauce with crème fraîche, a dash of Dijon mustard and some chopped leafy herbs such as dill, chives and flat-leaf parsley.

salmon en croûte with stem ginger and currants

100g unsalted butter, softened

4 knobs of stem ginger in syrup, finely chopped

30g currants

finely grated zest of 1 lemon, plus a couple of squeezes of juice

1 tablespoon finely chopped fresh tarragon leaves

1 shallot, peeled and finely chopped

sea salt, black pepper

1.2kg salmon fillet (skinned weight), in one piece

375g puff pastry

1 egg yolk, blended with 1 teaspoon water

Serves 6

Blend the butter in a bowl with the ginger, currants, lemon zest and juice, tarragon, shallot and some seasoning. Halve the salmon fillet horizontally. Season both sides of each piece, then spread half the butter over the top of one piece, sandwich with the other and spread the remaining butter on top of this.

Thinly roll out the pastry on a lightly floured work surface, and place the salmon in the centre, buttered side down. Trim the long edges so they are just large enough to enclose the salmon, then seal the parcel, painting the rim of the pastry with eggwash to secure it. Trim the ends, paint these with eggwash and fold in to secure. Place the parcel the right way up, and use the pastry trimmings to decorate it with leaves or a fish, securing them to the top with eggwash. Now paint the top all over with eggwash. The parcel can be made up to half a day in advance, in which case cover and chill it until required.

Preheat the oven to 200°C fan/220°C/gas mark 7 and bake the pie for about 40 minutes. Serve in slices.

gorgeous birds

Part of our French country Christmas as a family involves wandering down the lane and being heckled by our neighbours' turkeys as we pass. An elderly farming couple, they are typical of rural smallholders in Normandy who will rear a few turkeys in the run-up to Christmas. These birds lead as free a life as you could hope for, wandering from the shelter of a barn to the grass outside. They have rekindled my faith in the potential of turkey; at its finest the flesh is the palest pink, finely grained, succulent and almost gamey. Buy carefully and there is no reason why Christmas dinner should ever offer up less – today's well-reared bronze and rarer black turkeys are a world apart from the oversized birds bred for speed of growth that I grew up with.

Breed is not all, mind you, the cook plays a part. Going back a few years, the fashion for roasting a turkey was either to put it in to cook the night before, or to set the alarm for an hour or two before the cock crowed. Either way it was hours more than was required, so trust me on the timings here even if they do seem on the slim side of those you are accustomed to. Roasting the bird breast down will also make all the difference to keeping it succulent, allowing the fat and juices to trickle down into the flesh and baste it as it cooks.

For those who prefer to ring the changes from the norm, why not try pot-roast turkey, where the cooking juices keep the bird in fine succulent form and give you a ready-made gravy at the end? And if not turkey, there are any number of other birds that will be just as Christmassy dressed for the occasion, but that accommodate smaller numbers. Gatherings of two, three and four will almost certainly do better with a duck, a partridge, or even a goose. My ideal size of turkey is one up from that demanded by the occasion itself, and renders just enough left over for a retro turkey and ham pie, and of course some lovely soup.

By this stage of the game, the only thing you really want to know is how to get the dinner on the table with the minimum of possible fuss. It's hard enough juggling the trimmings without doing anything fancy with the bird. So this is your 'quick set-up guide'. However, if you do want to take the fancy route, the quatre épices butter provides a custom-made Christmas scent that gently infuses the turkey flesh as it cooks, while the butter bastes the breast – and it can be done in advance!

roast turkey

1 x 5kg turkey
25g unsalted butter, softened
sea salt, black pepper

Serves 8–10

the quick set-up guide

Preheat the oven to 200°C fan/220°C/gas mark 7. Stuff the turkey (see page 96–97), then rub the butter over the bird and season. Set the turkey breast side down in a large roasting tray. Protect the wings and legs with foil to prevent them from drying out. Place the turkey in the oven and roast for 30 minutes, then turn down to 180°C fan/200°C/gas mark 6 and continue roasting for the times suggested below (to include the 30 minutes).

Baste periodically with the juices in the roasting tray. About 30–45 minutes before the bird is cooked, turn it breast uppermost, removing the foil, so that it can brown. To check if the bird is cooked through, insert a skewer into the thickest part of the flesh (the thigh). The juices should run out clear. If not, give the bird another 10 minutes, then check again. Remove the turkey to a carving plate and leave it to rest for around 20 minutes while you make the gravy (see page 102–105). Carve the turkey and serve with the gravy.

roasting times

For a bird up to 5kg, allow 15 minutes per 500g.
For a bird over 5kg, allow 13 minutes per 500g.

roast turkey quatre épices

75g unsalted butter, softened
½ teaspoon each ground cinnamon,
    cloves, nutmeg, allspice
sea salt, black pepper
a bunch of fresh thyme or rosemary
zest of 1 lemon, removed with
    a potato peeler

Blend the butter with the spices and
some seasoning in a bowl. Starting at
the neck end, slip your fingers beneath
the skin to loosen it over each breast.
Spread the spiced butter underneath
the skin over the breasts and pat the
skin back into place, spreading the
butter out evenly. Pop the herbs and
lemon into the cavity. Cook as before.

This makes for a supremely succulent bird, and the gravy is part of the package, which is one less thing to worry about. By roasting the turkey on top of the giblets, you even have their lovely savour too. Use 'extra thick' foil for this, as it's less likely to tear or pierce.

pot-roast turkey with port gravy

1 lemon
50g unsalted butter, softened
1 tablespoon sliced fresh sage leaves
1 tablespoon fresh thyme leaves
sea salt, black pepper
1 x approx. 5kg turkey, untrussed,
  with giblets (reserve the livers for
  another time)
1 onion, peeled and sliced
vegetable oil
180ml port

Serves 8–10

roasting times

For a bird up to 5kg, allow 15 minutes per
  500g, plus 10 minutes over.
For a bird over 5kg, allow 13 minutes per
  500g, plus 20 minutes over.

Preheat the oven to 200°C fan/220°C/gas mark 7. Finely grate the lemon zest. Blend the butter, herbs, lemon zest and some seasoning in a bowl. Starting at the neck end of the turkey, slip your fingers beneath the skin to loosen it over each breast, breaking the membrane between them. Insert the herb butter, dividing it between the breasts, and pat the skin to spread the butter out evenly. Roll the lemon on the work surface, prick it all over, and pop it into the neck cavity, tucking the flap of skin underneath.

Place the turkey on top of the giblets and the onion in a large roasting dish that holds the bird quite snugly. Lightly oil the turkey and season it with salt and pepper. Pour 500ml of water into the base of the dish and cover with foil. The dish should be airtight, leaving enough room for the bird to stretch as it cooks without piercing the foil. Basically, you will need to pleat several lengths of foil together, with enough spare to tuck underneath the dish. If the foil isn't totally secured, the steam created inside will lift it off during roasting. Roast for 30 minutes, then turn the oven down to 180°C fan/200°C/gas mark 6 and continue to roast for the times suggested below.

Forty-five minutes before the end of cooking, remove the foil. There should still be a good pool of liquid in the base, but if not, add a little more water. Add the port, baste and return the bird to the oven to brown. To check if the bird is cooked through, insert a skewer into the thickest part of the thigh – the juices should run out clear. If not, and if they appear bloody or pink, give the bird another 15 minutes, then check again.

Transfer the turkey to a carving plate to rest for 20 minutes, loosely covering it with foil. Simmer the gravy on the hob until it tastes well-balanced, then pass it through a sieve into a jug. Add any juices given out on carving the bird.

Turkey breasts come off the bone and on, when they are known as a crown roast. I like to buy mine boned and rolled and to stuff it myself, as here, where the leeks provide a buttery succulence, and the porcini work their perfumed magic, and you get crispy bacon on the outside to boot.

stuffed roast turkey breast with cranberry gravy

Stuffing

115g unsalted butter

5 leeks (600g trimmed weight), sliced

sea salt, black pepper

40g dried porcini, soaked in 300ml
   boiling water for 30 minutes

2 tablespoons chopped fresh
   flat-leaf parsley

finely grated zest of 1 lemon,
   plus a squeeze of juice

80g unsweetened brioche

2 medium egg yolks

300ml rich chicken stock

Turkey and Gravy

1.5kg turkey breast, boned and rolled

5 rashers of rindless unsmoked
   streaky bacon

sea salt, black pepper

6 tablespoons port

1 tablespoon cranberry sauce

Serves 6

To make the stuffing* melt 50g of the butter in a large frying pan over a medium heat, add the leeks, season them and cook gently for 12–15 minutes until soft and lightly coloured, stirring occasionally. Transfer them to a bowl. Drain and finely chop the porcini, reserving the liquor. Stir the mushrooms into the leeks together with the parsley, lemon zest and juice. Leaving the crusts on the brioche, reduce it to fine crumbs in a food processor and stir these into the stuffing. Add the egg yolks and blend using a wooden spoon. The stuffing can be prepared to this point several hours in advance, in which case cover and set it aside in a cool place.

Preheat the oven to 190°C fan/210°C/gas mark 6. Snip the string binding the turkey breast and slip the ties off. Lay the bacon rashers in a row on the chopping board about 2–3cm apart, and lay the turkey breast skin down on top. Open out the pocket of the breast and stuff with about a third of the stuffing. Bring the bacon slices up around the sides and tie it up again, wrapping a piece of string around each rasher of bacon to secure it. Season it on both sides with salt and pepper and place skin side up in a roasting dish that holds it snugly. Dot with 50g of the butter, pour over the reserved mushroom soaking liquor and roast for 18 minutes per 500g (including the weight of the stuffing). Baste the joint a couple of times in the course of roasting, adding a drop more water or chicken stock to the roasting dish towards the end if the juices get too syrupy.

Shape the remaining stuffing into balls the size of a plum and arrange in a shallow ovenproof dish, spaced about 1cm apart. Pour half the chicken stock into the base of the baking dish to a depth of a few millimetres, dot the stuffing balls with the remaining 15g of butter and roast for 30–35 minutes, until lightly golden (i.e. putting them into the oven about 10 minutes before the turkey is ready to allow for it resting).

Once the turkey is cooked, transfer the joint and any stuffing on the bottom of the dish to a warm carving plate, loosely cover with foil and leave to rest for 20 minutes. Skim any excess fat from the roasting dish, add the port and simmer to reduce by half, scraping up all the sticky bits. Stir in the cranberry sauce and once the jelly has melted blend in the rest of the stock. Simmer for a few minutes, until it tastes nice and rich. Taste and add a little more seasoning if necessary. Carve the turkey, adding any juices given out to the gravy.

*If you prefer you could make all the stuffing into balls, in which case dot with 25g of butter and pour over 200ml stock.

roast goose with prune and apple stuffing

A plump roast goose with its crackly parchment-crisp skin and succulent dark flesh goes unsurpassed. I enjoy it best stuffed with prunes and apples, and served with some small crispy potatoes (see page 80) and a pile of watercress or other green leaves. Maybe the luxury of a bread sauce thrown in, but no more than that. In fact it's so easy to prepare I always stand around thinking I must have forgotten something.

Although goose has a reputation for being meaner than a turkey, a 4.5kg bird does nicely for six, and the average oven will accommodate up to 5.3kg. One of the great joys in roasting a goose is the copious golden fat given off, which makes for superlative roast and sauté potatoes. Any fat that comes separately with the giblets, or that you remove from the bird's cavity, can also be put to use. Gently heat it in a small frying pan or saucepan, strain, and bottle it in a wide-necked jar. It keeps almost indefinitely in the fridge.

Whereas we usually base gravy on the roasting juices in the bottom of the pan, with goose it is better to play safe and prepare it using the giblets. You can include the goose liver in this line-up, though there again it's such a delicacy you may like to keep it for a treat the next day. The gravy can also be made in advance and reheated.

Stuffing

250g ready-to-eat stoned prunes
225ml port
25g unsalted butter
450g Bramley apples, peeled,
     cored and diced
1 tablespoon caster sugar

Goose

1 x 4.5kg goose, with giblets
groundnut oil
sea salt, black pepper
watercress to serve 6
1 x quantity of bread sauce,
     optional (see page 101)

Gravy

100ml port
1 teaspoon plain flour, sifted
400ml giblet stock (see page 104)

Serves 6

To make the stuffing, place the prunes in a small saucepan with the port. Bring to the boil, then simmer over a low heat for 15–20 minutes until all but a tablespoon of syrupy liquid remains, stirring towards the end. At the same time, melt the butter in a large frying pan over a medium heat, add the apples and sauté for about 5 minutes, stirring frequently, until lightly coloured and just beginning to lose their shape. Sprinkle over the sugar and cook for a minute or so longer until you have the beginnings of an apple sauce, with whole pieces still evident. Combine the prunes and residual syrup with the apples in a bowl, cover with a plate or clingfilm and leave to cool. Chill if preparing more than a few hours in advance of using.

Preheat the oven to 200°C fan/220°C/gas mark 7. Place a rack in a baking tray that contains a few millimetres of water in the bottom (see page 9). Place two large sheets of foil on top of the rack, overlapping widthways, and pierce so that the fat can drain through. Remove any surplus fat at the entrance to the body cavity of the goose. Leaving the bird trussed, spoon the stuffing into the cavity, pushing it well back.

Rub the goose all over with oil and season. Prick the skin and fat gland under each wing. Cover the legs with some of the surplus fat and wrap them in foil. Place the goose breast side up on the foil and wrap it into a parcel.

Cook the goose for 16–17 minutes per 500g, therefore 2½ hours for a 4.5kg goose. Roast for 30 minutes, then turn the oven down to 180°C fan/200°C/gas mark 6. A third of the way into cooking, unwrap and remove the foil, leaving the legs covered. Drain off any excess fat, reserving it for later, turn the goose breast down and roast for another third of the total time. Turn the goose breast up again, draining off any more excess fat, and roast for the remainder of the cooking time. Transfer the goose to a warm serving plate, loosely cover with foil and leave to rest for 30 minutes.

Skim any excess fat from the giblet roasting dish, add the port and simmer on the hob until well reduced. Stir in the flour, dispersing any lumps with the back of the spoon, and once this is seething gradually stir in the stock. Simmer the gravy long and hard enough for it to amalgamate into a smooth sauce. Taste and season if necessary. Pass through a sieve into a jug to serve. Carve the goose and serve with a spoonful of the stuffing and a pile of watercress. Serve the gravy and any bread sauce separately at the table.

A classically gorgeous scenario of ingredients that go together hand in glove. Under normal circumstances, two people will make light work of a duck, but eaten with black pudding it will spread to four. I usually serve small baked potatoes with this, but sauté potatoes are just as good. I would make a big jug of 'extra gravy' (see page 102) to go with this. Duck benefits from a long slow roasting, the surest way of ensuring crisp golden skin, and farmed duck is preferable to wild here.

roast duck with black pudding and apple

Duck

1 x 2.5kg duck, oven-ready

sea salt

a handful each of fresh sage leaves,
   oregano sprigs and thyme sprigs

Dressing

2 eating apples, peeled, cored and sliced

8 x 1cm slices of black pudding

watercress to serve 4

Serves 4

Preheat the oven to 180°C fan/200°C/gas mark 6. Prick the duck skin all over with a skewer and generously rub with salt. Stuff the cavity of the duck with the herbs. Place the duck breast side up on a rack within a roasting tray and roast for 1 hour (see page 9). Drain the fat into a bowl, turn the oven down to 150°C fan/170°C/gas mark 3, and roast for a further 1½ hours, draining it a second time halfway through. Remove the duck to a warm plate, loosely cover it with foil and leave to rest for 20 minutes.

While the duck is resting, heat 2 tablespoons of the duck fat in a large frying pan over a highish heat and sauté the apples for about 6 minutes, turning them now and again until golden on both sides. Transfer them to a warm plate, add another tablespoon of duck fat to the pan and colour the black pudding slices for about 1 minute on either side. Serve the roast duck with the black pudding and apple, some gravy and a pile of watercress.

The traditional line-up for grouse of bread sauce, buttery crumbs and watercress is just as good with other game birds. A grey partridge for me steals the show with its tender gaminess. It does one for one, which makes it ideal when it's just two, three or four of you. I would make a big jug of 'extra gravy' (see page 102) to go with this.

partridge that thinks it's a grouse

Partridge

4 grey-leg partridges, oven-ready,
   untrussed
50g unsalted butter, softened
sea salt, black pepper
8 rashers of rindless unsmoked
   streaky bacon

Dressing and Crumbs

150g unsalted butter
150g fresh white breadcrumbs
1 x quantity of bread sauce (see
   page 101)
redcurrant jelly or other game sauce
   to serve
watercress to serve 4

Serves 4

Preheat the oven to 200°C fan/220°C/gas mark 7. Smear the birds with the butter, season them with pepper and the tiniest pinch of salt, then wrap two rashers of bacon around each bird, one securing the legs. Place in a roasting dish about 1cm apart and roast for 30 minutes, basting halfway through. Transfer the birds to a warm serving plate to rest for 10 minutes. If you want your bacon extra crispy, unwrap the bacon rashers and lay these out in another small baking dish, then return this to the oven to crisp for a few minutes while the bird is resting.

To make the crumbs, melt the butter in a large frying pan over a medium heat and once it is sizzling nicely add the breadcrumbs and fry, stirring frequently, until they are evenly gold – this may take up to 15 minutes, depending on how fresh the crumbs are. Spread them in a thin layer on a double thickness of kitchen paper to drain for a few minutes, then transfer to a bowl. They can be made up to about an hour in advance, but keep them somewhere warm in the kitchen so they remain feathery light and the butter doesn't set.

Just before eating, gently rewarm the bread sauce, spoon it into a bowl and serve separately at the table with the game crumbs and the redcurrant jelly. Accompany each partridge with the bacon and a small bunch of watercress.

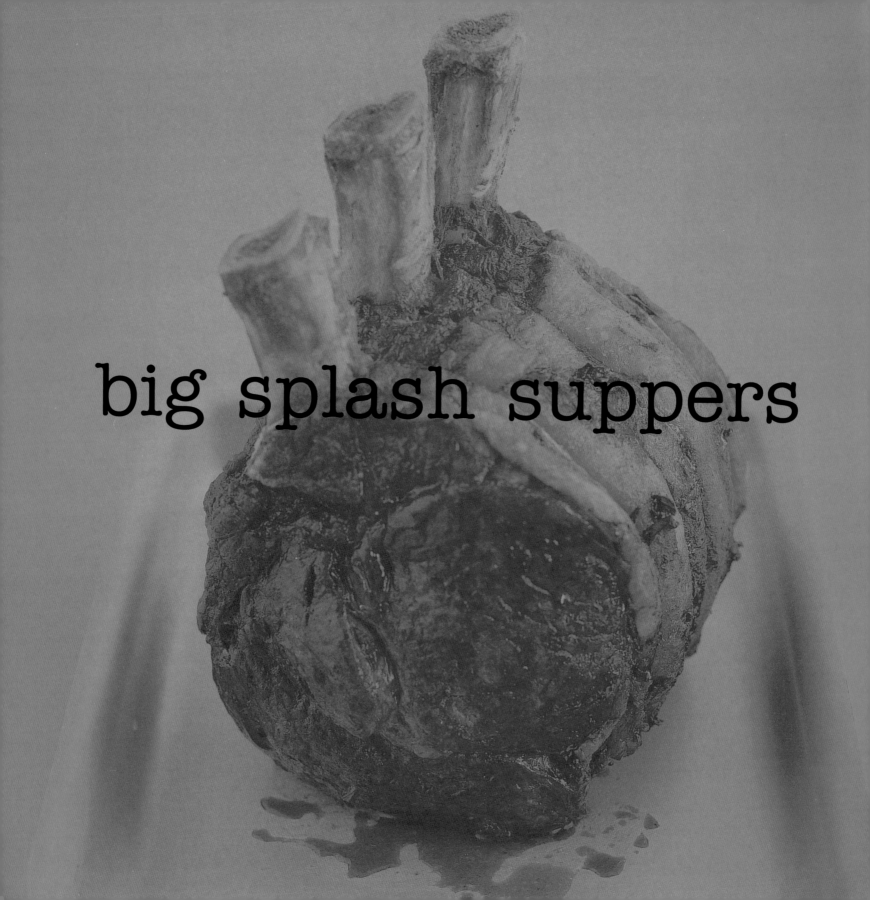

The feasting proper in our house begins on Christmas Eve. Traditionally we roast up a whole turbot, which is as easy as it is spectacular. In France, where we always spend Christmas, seafood is a big part of the *reveillon*, the traditional Christmas Eve dinner, so fishmongers are every bit as lavishly decked out as the butcher, the slab laid out with beautiful specimens. Turbot is an obvious treat, but a whole brill, a close relation, won't let you down and neither will a large plaice or two. And for those who want to avoid turkey and its ilk on the day, a rib of beef or fillet steak en croute makes for a fine alternative.

A ham at Christmas is for most as essential to the celebrations as the tree and the turkey. As such it is possessed of a culture of its own; the pickles, mustardy sauces and spiced fruits that go hand in hand, and the sandwiches that can be made with the proceeds, are a treat to be anticipated in the days that follow. Plan it right and it can span several days, first eaten hot with a parsley sauce, and thereafter cold. The third delight is the stock left over from boiling the ham or made with the proceeds of the bone on which it was cooked – with the addition of a few modest vegetables, some pearl barley and strips of ham it can be turned into a warming feast.

The most popular cut of gammon (an uncooked ham) is the leg, which comes on the bone, or boned and rolled. The latter can be obtained in almost any size, though a 2kg joint will do nicely for eight people and just fit your biggest saucepan, and should promise to be beautifully succulent. A knuckle-end gammon joint (half leg on the bone) is good for ten plus. Good butchers, some of whom cure their own gammons, will be able to advise on whether you need to soak your gammon overnight; if however you are buying from a supermarket I would recommend soaking the gammon as a matter of course. As to unsmoked or smoked, it's a question of taste, and your preference in bacon should steer the course.

This juicy joint of ham with a sticky glaze can be served hot, with a creamy gravy made with the basting juices, but as ever it's just as good cold. Ham, like turkey, is a dinner of several lives, and it seems a shame not to cook up a joint that will give you plenty to carve in the days to come. Gammon from the middle cut of leg can come up wide and thin, so for ease of carving aim for a joint some 15cm long, about 12cm in diameter.

earl grey ham

1 x 2.5–2.8kg unsmoked gammon,
   boned and rolled
3 outer sticks of celery, trimmed
   and sliced
2 carrots, trimmed and sliced
1 leek, trimmed and sliced
2 bay leaves
1½ tablespoons wholegrain mustard
50g dark muscovado sugar
approx. 400ml strong Earl Grey tea
150g crème fraîche

Serves 8–10

Consult your butcher, and if necessary soak the gammon in cold water overnight, then drain. Place the gammon in a large saucepan, cover with cold water and bring to the boil. Discard the water and start again with fresh water to cover, this time adding the chopped vegetables and bay leaves. Bring to the boil, and maintain at a gentle simmer, topping up with boiling water if necessary. Calculate the cooking time at 40 minutes per kilo, subtracting 35 minutes for glazing it in the oven. So a 3kg joint will need 1 hour 25 minutes boiling.

Preheat the oven to 200°C fan/220°C/gas mark 7. Transfer the ham from the saucepan on to a board using two forks. Remove any string and paper around it, and pull or cut off the rind if present. Slash the fat at 2cm intervals in a crisscross pattern, without going down as far as the meat. It is a good idea to skewer the opening where the bone was with a couple of metal skewers, one going each way, so the ham doesn't unravel in the oven.

Brush the fat with the mustard, then press the sugar on top. Place the ham fat side up in a roasting dish and pour 400ml of tea into the base. Roast for 30–35 minutes, until the glaze is sticky and caramelised. Baste the ham halfway through, adding a little more tea if you think it's reducing too quickly – there should be a pool of rich golden juices at the end. Transfer the ham to a serving plate, and leave to rest for 20 minutes. Add the crème fraîche to the juices and simmer until rich and amalgamated. Remove the skewers, carve and serve the ham with the sauce. You can also reheat the sliced ham in the sauce at a later date, a useful one for all those teenagers traipsing back from the pub.

This is a lovely sticky aromatic glaze that makes a change from the norm, and the pan juices can be eked out, with the addition of a little cream, to give you a rich sauce for serving it hot. You could also add some finely chopped parsley.

sherry and quince-glazed ham

1 x 3.5kg knuckle-end smoked
   gammon joint on the bone
150g quince paste or jelly (membrillo)
3 tablespoons wholegrain mustard
50ml medium sherry
approx. 40 cloves
100ml whipping cream

Serves 10

Consult your butcher, and if necessary soak the gammon in cold water overnight, then drain.

Preheat the oven to 170°C fan/190°C/gas mark 5. Try to use the broadest width of foil. Tear off a long sheet, large enough to envelop the gammon, allowing plenty of air within the package to circulate. If the foil isn't wide enough, pleat the edges of two or three lengths together to create one large piece. Place the gammon on top, bring the long sides together, fold to seal them, then do the same with the sides. Place the gammon in a roasting dish or grill pan. It needs to bake for 60 minutes per kilo, so calculate it accordingly, subtracting 30 minutes for the final glazing. A 3.5kg gammon will need to bake for 3 hours prior to glazing.

Just before the end, gently heat the quince paste or jelly in a small saucepan, working it with a wooden spoon until it thins. Transfer to a bowl and blend in first the mustard and then the sherry. Remove the ham from the oven and turn the temperature up to 180°C fan/200°C/gas mark 6. Unwrap the ham and slip out the foil, then slice off the rind underneath the ham, which will have softened in the cooking juices, leaving behind as much of the fat as possible. Next carefully incise a long slit into the rind across the top without cutting into the fat – you can use scissors for this – and partly pull and partly cut the skin off. Use oven gloves or a tea towel to protect your hands from getting burnt.

Glaze the top and sides of the ham as evenly as possible with the quince-sherry glaze. Slice the fat at 2cm intervals with a crisscross pattern and insert cloves into the crosses on the fat.

Return the ham to the roasting dish or grill pan and pour a few millimetres of water into the base to prevent any glaze on the base from burning. Roast for 25–30 minutes, until the glaze is golden and dry, checking it halfway through and adding a little more water if necessary. Transfer the ham to a warm serving plate, loosely cover with foil and leave to rest for 30 minutes.

If serving the ham hot, skim the fat off the juices in the roasting dish, add 150–200ml of water and simmer for a few minutes, scraping up the residue on the bottom of the pan, then add the cream and simmer for a few minutes longer. Add any juices given out on resting the ham. To serve, moisten the meat with just a couple of spoons of the sauce, which is quite rich.

If serving the ham cold, place it somewhere cool or unheated and leave to cool completely. A larder makes the ideal environment for storing a cooked ham; basically it should be somewhere cool and slightly damp – a garage is an alternative. It will keep well for about a week, or if it has been sliced then 3 days. You can reheat slices of ham in the sauce in the days to follow. First skim off any fat that has risen to the surface of the sauce on chilling.

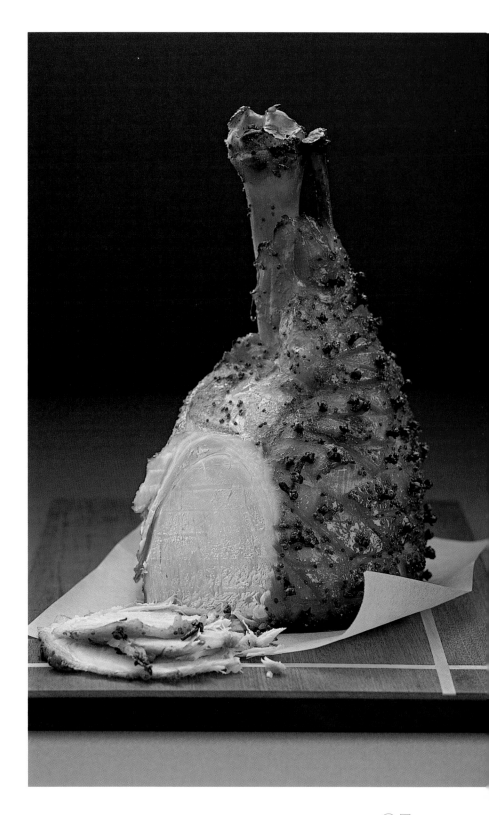

Turbot has beautifully sweet white milky flesh, and roasting it on the bone ensures it remains succulent. Any tattie of choice will be good here, buttery mash or boiled with lots of salted butter, and a big green salad.

whole roasted turbot

2 lemons, sliced, ends discarded
extra virgin olive oil
1 x approx. 2kg whole turbot
sea salt, black pepper
1 tablespoon soft fresh thyme leaves
1 tablespoon fresh rosemary needles
150ml white wine
30g unsalted butter

Serves 4

Preheat the oven to 200°C fan/220°C/gas mark 7. Heat a large non-stick frying pan over a medium-high heat. Brush the lemon slices with oil on both sides and sear these for about 1 minute each side, until coloured. Score the flesh of both sides of the turbot quite deeply, diagonally at 5cm intervals. Season the slits well on both sides with salt and pepper, then stuff them with a pinch of the thyme and rosemary. Place the fish underside down in a roasting dish or grill pan. Pour on the wine, then lay over the lemon slices and dot with the butter.

Roast for 30–35 minutes, until the flesh is just cooked. It should have lost its translucency and come away from the bone with ease.

A fab centrepiece for any dinner, buffet or sit-down. Because a rib of beef takes up most of the oven, I prefer to serve mashed rather than roast potatoes – the Christmas champ on page 83 should do you proud. Jars of preserved grated fresh horseradish will stand in for fresh should it prove hard to come by. Start by adding 2 tablespoons of horseradish to the crème fraîche, then taste it and add more if you like it hotter.

roast rib of beef with horseradish sauce

Beef

1 x 3-bone rib of beef, oven-ready
½ teaspoon plain flour, plus
    1 tablespoon
½ teaspoon English mustard powder
75ml port
½ teaspoon Dijon mustard
400ml beef stock
sea salt, black pepper

Sauce

200g crème fraîche
2–3 tablespoons finely grated
    horseradish

Serves 6

Take your joint out of the fridge an hour before roasting to allow it to come up to room temperature. Preheat the oven to 240°C fan/260°C/gas mark 10 (if your oven doesn't go that high, preheat it to its highest setting), and place the rib fat side up in a roasting tray that holds it snugly. Sift the ½ teaspoon of flour and the ½ teaspoon of mustard together, and dust this over the fat using a tea strainer or fine mesh sieve.

Roast the joint for 20 minutes, then turn the oven down to 180°C fan/200°C/ gas mark 6, allowing 12 minutes per 500g for rare meat, and 15 minutes for medium rare. Baste the joint every 20–30 minutes.

To make the sauce, blend the crème fraîche and horseradish together and season with salt. Transfer to a clean bowl, cover and chill until required.

Once cooked, transfer the joint to a serving plate and leave to rest for 20 minutes out of the oven, loosely covered with foil. Skim any excess fat off the roasting tray. Add the port and cook for a few minutes, scraping up all the sticky bits on the bottom, until well reduced. Stir in the Dijon mustard and the tablespoon of flour, then thin it with the beef stock and simmer for several minutes. Taste to check the seasoning, and pass through a sieve into a jug or bowl. Carve the roast and add any juices given out during the process of carving to the gravy. Serve the horseradish sauce separately at the table.

This remains the chicest party piece, hot or cold, and with the plethora of wild mushrooms available to us the results promise to be better than ever. Although fillet is undeniably expensive, you don't need quite as much as you would if eating another cut of steak. I would dish this up with some small crispy potatoes and mustard.

fillet steak en croûte

300g wild and cultivated
  mushrooms, picked over
  and trimmed
25g unsalted butter
2 shallots, peeled and finely chopped
sea salt, black pepper
2 tablespoons chopped fresh
  flat-leaf parsley
a squeeze of lemon juice
750g piece of fillet steak, trimmed
  of fat and sinew (ask your butcher
  for the thick end of the fillet)
groundnut oil
350–400g puff pastry
100g cream cheese
1 scant tablespoon Dijon mustard,
  plus extra to serve
1 medium egg, beaten

Serves 4–6

Finely chop the mushrooms by hand into pieces a few millimetres in size. Melt the butter in a large frying pan over a medium heat, add the shallots and sweat for a few minutes until softened, stirring them occasionally. Add the mushrooms and some seasoning and continue to fry for another 5–6 minutes, until any juices given out have evaporated and they have started to colour. Transfer them to a bowl, stir in the parsley and lemon juice and leave to cool.

Heat another large frying pan over a medium heat for several minutes. Brush the fillet steak all over with oil, season it and sear for 1 minute on each side. Transfer to a plate and leave to cool.

Thinly roll out the pastry on a lightly floured work surface. Spread the cream cheese over the middle, to cover an area the size of the fillet. Spread the mushrooms on top. Brush the top of the fillet with the mustard and place, mustard-side down, on top of the mushrooms. Trim the pastry, allowing enough to parcel up the steak. Paint one of the long edges and both short sides with the beaten egg. Bring the long painted edge up over the other long edge, then tuck up the sides, trimming off any excess pastry and securing them with more egg wash. Place on a baking tray, sealed edges down, and use the trimmings to decorate the top of the pie, fixing them with the beaten egg. You can prepare the steak to this point a couple of hours in advance, cover and chill it.

Preheat the oven to 220°C fan/240°C/gas mark 9. Brush the croûte all over with the beaten egg and bake for 30 minutes, until golden. Leave to rest for 10 minutes, then carve into thick slices; don't worry if this seems rather messy. The end slices will be medium rare and the centre ones rare. Accompany with extra mustard.

This rings the changes from the traditional Christmas palette, but is as festive as any other big roast, and anything pot-roasted makes for ease, with lashings of ready-made gravy that is so central to a pot of mash or buttery spuds. There is no need to forgo the crackling either. Ask your butcher to slice off the rind, so that the fat is evenly distributed between fat and skin, score and roast it separately.

slow-roast pork shoulder with fennel and anchovies

Pork

1½ teaspoons fennel seeds,
   coarsely ground

1/3 teaspoon dried chilli flakes

2kg boned and rolled shoulder of pork,
   rind removed and scored

sea salt

1 tablespoon extra virgin olive oil

½ bottle of white wine

380ml chicken stock

7 salted anchovy fillets, sliced

3 garlic cloves, peeled and smashed

Fennel

4 fennel bulbs, shoots and outer sheath
   discarded, cut into thin wedges

150ml chicken stock

150ml white wine

25g unsalted butter, diced

sea salt, black pepper

Serves 6

Preheat the oven to 140°C fan/160°C/gas mark 2½. Rub the fennel seeds and chilli over the pork (don't worry about the ends), and season with salt. Heat the oil in a large frying pan over a medium-high heat and colour the pork all over, then place it, fat side down, into a large cast-iron casserole. Add the wine, stock, anchovies and garlic. Bring to the boil, then cover and place in the oven for 5 hours, turning it halfway through. At the same time, rub some salt into the pork skin, place it skin side up in a small roasting dish and place in the oven.

Shortly before removing the pork from the oven, place all the ingredients for the fennel in a medium-size saucepan and bring to the boil. Cover the pan and cook for 30 minutes, until the fennel is meltingly tender, stirring halfway through, then drain.

When the 5 hours is up, transfer the pork to a plate to rest for 20 minutes, loosely covered with foil. Turn the oven up to 220°C fan/240°C/gas mark 9 to crisp the crackling while the meat is resting – it should turn pale, with small bubbles below the surface. Skim the fat off the roasting juices (you may find it easiest to pour these into a glass jug first and then return them to the pan). Simmer to reduce by about a third, until well flavoured.

The meat should be meltingly tender and you should be able to just pull it apart with a fork and spoon. Serve with the juices, the fennel and the crackling.

Squash come in many different shapes and sizes. Kabocha, Baby Squash and Harlequin are shaped like baby pumpkins and are ideal for stuffing. The latter are too pretty to miss on the Christmas table, and true to their name are patched with orange and green streaks. You could also stuff these the night before, and chill them overnight.

baked squash with wild mushrooms, apple and chestnuts

2 x squash (approx. 700g)

50g unsalted butter, plus extra
   to serve

3 shallots, peeled and finely chopped

150g wild mushrooms, picked over
   and torn or sliced as necessary

1 eating apple, peeled, cored
   and diced

sea salt, black pepper

75g cooked and peeled chestnuts,
   coarsely chopped

1 tablespoon fresh marjoram or
   thyme leaves

Serves 6

Preheat the oven to 180°C fan/200°C/gas mark 6. The squash need to stand level without rolling around, so if necessary nick off a slice from the base. Cut off the tops and scoop out the seeds inside.

Melt the 50g of butter in a large frying pan over a medium heat. Add the shallots and cook for a minute or two until softened, stirring occasionally, then add the mushrooms and apple and sauté for a few minutes longer, until the mushrooms are cooked and the apple is translucent and starting to colour. Season, then add the chestnuts and marjoram or thyme and cook for a minute longer.

Season the inside of the squash generously with salt and pepper and stuff with the mushroom and apple mixture, pressing it well down. Replace the lids, place the squash in a baking dish and roast for 1 hour. To serve, scoop out the stuffing and the squash flesh. You may like to arrange this in a dish and dot with some butter to serve.

A lovely chicken curry is a winner around Christmas and New Year. This one is mild and fragrant. I would serve it spooned over buttered spinach, accompanied by mini naan breads warmed in the oven for a few minutes, as well as a big pot of rice. Any luxury cocktail nut will do here, such as roasted almonds or salt and pepper cashews.

saffron butter chicken korma

50g unsalted butter

sea salt, black pepper

8 chicken thighs

2 onions, peeled, halved and
   thinly sliced

2 garlic cloves, peeled and
   finely chopped

2cm fresh ginger, peeled and
   finely chopped

2 medium-hot fresh red chillies

1 bay leaf

1 x 7cm cinnamon stick

8 cloves

6 green cardamom pods, smashed
   with the bottom of a glass or a
   rolling pin

approx. 25 saffron filaments

1 teaspoon cornflour

300ml natural yoghurt

chopped fresh coriander and roast
   pistachios to serve (optional)

a little chicken stock (if reheating)

Serves 4

Gently melt the butter in a small saucepan, skim off the surface foam, decant the clarified butter and discard the milky solids below. Heat the clarified butter in a large cast-iron casserole over a medium heat. Season the chicken thighs on both sides and colour the flesh side for about 7 minutes until nicely golden, then turn and colour the skin side for about another 7 minutes, again until nicely golden.

Transfer the chicken to a bowl, add the onions, garlic, ginger, chillies, bay leaf and spices, and fry for another few minutes, until the onions are softened and starting to colour. Return the chicken to the pan, placing it skin down and nestling it between the onions and spices. Cover the pan and cook over a low heat for 30 minutes until the chicken is tender and comes away from the bone with ease.

Blend the cornflour with a tablespoon of water in a medium-size bowl, then gradually blend in the yoghurt. Transfer the chicken thighs to a serving dish and keep warm. Skim the fat off the cooking juices, stir in the yoghurt and heat gently. The cornflour will stabilise the sauce and prevent it from splitting if it boils. Taste, then spoon the sauce over the chicken thighs and scatter with coriander and pistachios if liked. You can pick out the whole spices as you eat. If you want to make it in advance and reheat it, you will probably need to thin the sauce with a little chicken stock.

all the trimmings

Who could possibly resist all the little asides that come with the turkey, the trimmings as they are fondly known, however many or excessive they may be? It's the pick 'n' mix that defines Christmas dinner: a fork piled with a small sprout, a dab of bread sauce, a sliver of bacon roll and chipolata, followed by another of turkey with a little cranberry sauce and a morsel of stuffing. The potentially gorgeous forkfuls are endless, so don't let's be too hard on ourselves for the lack of discipline in paring it down.

My own menu runs something like this: turkey with a sage and onion stuffing, sausage and chipolata rolls, roast potatoes, parsnips with Parmesan, sprouts with chestnuts, bread and cranberry sauce, and a huge jug of gravy. Some people also like to serve ham at the same time as the turkey, though I usually wait until Boxing Day for this one. I try to get well ahead on Christmas Eve, so there's no more than a couple of hours to be spent bringing it all together on the day, a peaceful time in the kitchen late afternoon when there's a lull in the presents and partying. We normally eat in the evening, around eight or nine, but I know lots of people who go for a late afternoon dinner around four o'clock. It's one of those meals you can serve any time that suits you lunchtime onwards.

And part of the excess is having lots of leftovers to carry you through the days to come. There is little more enjoyable on Boxing Day than grazing on a turkey that's been cooling in the larder, with all the leftover trimmings. Turkey and bread sauce sandwiches are heaven, as is turkey with jellied gravy, or a cold chipolata and bacon roll dipped into the cranberry sauce. Boxing Day lunch takes care of itself. And once that's over, the turkey has yet another lease of life as a rich golden stock, and a retro turkey and ham pie. So think of 'all the trimmings' as an investment, a promise of some feet-up time for the poor cook.

The best roasties are all crispy shell with just a little fluffy potato within, which means cutting them small. As well as roasting them in butter, goose fat makes for fab results, and olive oil is a promise of super-crisp tatties too. The main consideration is the potatoes themselves: King Edward and Maris Piper are reliable varieties that will turn meltingly soft within, and both have a lovely flavour.

roast potatoes

1.5kg maincrop potatoes
120–150g unsalted butter, melted
sea salt

Serves 6

Preheat the oven to 180°C fan/200°C/gas mark 6. Peel and cut up your potatoes and reserve in a bowl of cold water. Bring a large pan of salted water to the boil. Add the potatoes to the pan and cook for 8 minutes. Drain the potatoes into a sieve and leave for a minute or two for the surface water to evaporate. Return them to the pan and roughly shake it from side to side, tossing them until they appear textured and floury on the surface.

Tip them into a roasting tray, trickle over the butter and scatter over some sea salt. Roast the potatoes for 1 hour and 15 minutes, turning them at least once during cooking. They should be evenly gold all over, the colour of a crisp.

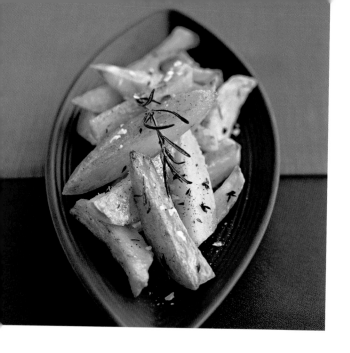

When the call is for chips but you want something that little bit more sophisticated, these will get wolfed down regardless of what you serve them with. If you are increasing the quantity, however, you will need to use either a proportionately bigger tray, or two, to ensure the chips colour and crisp evenly.

oven-roasted chips with rosemary and thyme

1.2kg large waxy potatoes, peeled
10 sprigs of fresh thyme
5 small sprigs of fresh rosemary
finely grated zest of 1 lemon, plus 1
   tablespoon lemon juice
2 tablespoons extra virgin olive oil
40g unsalted butter
sea salt, black pepper

Serves 4–6

Preheat the oven to 180°C fan/200°C/gas mark 6. Slice the potatoes lengthways 1cm thick, then cut these slices into thick chips. Arrange them in a 38 x 25cm roasting dish with the thyme, rosemary and lemon zest. Drizzle over the olive oil and lemon juice, dot with the butter and season. Cover with foil and roast for 25 minutes. Loosen the chips with a spatula and give them a stir, then roast uncovered for another 45–55 minutes until deliciously golden and caramelised, giving them another stir 10–15 minutes before the end.

A lovely lavish chestnut and potato mash that can be dished up at any number of occasions over the festive period, with the turkey, or with roast ham, pork or beef. It can be made in advance and gently reheated, which makes it perfect buffet material. Being prepared on the hob, it's also a good one for big splash joints and birds that are likely to dominate the oven, leaving no room for roast potatoes.

christmas champ

900g maincrop potatoes,
    peeled and cut up
250g unsweetened chestnut purée
    (about 2/3 of a 400g tin)
3 bunches of spring onions
    (approx. 400g), trimmed
100g unsalted butter, plus a
    knob to serve
200ml double cream
sea salt, black pepper
freshly grated nutmeg

Serves 6

Bring a large pan of salted water to the boil and cook the potatoes for 20–25 minutes until tender. Drain, leave to steam dry, then press them through a mouli-légumes back into the saucepan. Whiz the chestnut purée in a food processor until it is really soft and creamy. Blend this with the potato. At the same time as cooking the potatoes, cut the spring onions into 1cm slices including the green parts. Melt the butter in a medium or large saucepan over a medium heat, and cook the onion for about 5 minutes until it is soft and silky, stirring occasionally. Add the cream and season with salt, pepper and nutmeg, bring to a simmer and cook for another few minutes until the mixture thickens.

Stir two-thirds of the cream and onion into the purée and adjust the seasoning. If making this in advance, cover the surface of the mash and the remaining sauce with clingfilm and set aside. Just before serving, if necessary gently reheat the purée and the reserved sauce. Spoon the potato purée into a serving bowl, pour the sauce on top and turn it over a few times to loosely mix it in – most of the cream should remain on the surface. Make a well in the centre and drop in the remaining knob of butter.

This recipe was given to me by Jo Higgo, a friend who lives down the road from us in France, and I have never cooked parsnips any other way at Christmas since first tasting hers. The Parmesan cooks to a delicious toasty crisp that covers the parsnips.

parmesan-glazed parsnips

600g parsnips, trimmed and peeled,
  halved lengthways and cut into
  2 shorter lengths
50g unsalted butter, melted
30g freshly grated Parmesan
black pepper

Serves 4–6

Heat the oven to 180°C fan/200°C/gas mark 6 and bring a large pan of salted water to the boil. Add the parsnips and cook for 8 minutes, then drain them in a colander and leave for a few minutes to steam dry. Place them in a roasting dish, drizzle over the butter, shake a little from side to side to coat them, then sprinkle over the Parmesan and season with pepper. Roast for 40–45 minutes, until the cheese is golden and crisp, basting and loosening them with a spatula halfway through. Serve straight away.

Brussels sprouts are a small oasis of green in an otherwise X-rated dinner. My family, shame on them, agree to eat one each, which makes for a lot of leftovers, but I'm not prepared to give up. Personally I think sprouts are a different vegetable when they're fried, the outside turning delicately crisp and sweet.

Don't worry about including the bacon nibs if you're already doing bacon-wrapped chipolatas – simply fry the chestnuts with the sprouts. The vac-pacs or tins of cooked and peeled chestnuts come into their own here.

brussels sprouts with bacon and chestnuts

700g button Brussels sprouts, base trimmed and outer leaves discarded

8 rashers of rindless unsmoked streaky bacon, diced

100g cooked and peeled chestnuts, sliced

40g unsalted butter

sea salt, black pepper

Serves 6–8

Bring a large pan of salted water to the boil. Add the sprouts and cook for about 8 minutes, until just tender; larger sprouts will take longer accordingly. Drain in a colander.

Heat a large dry frying pan over a medium heat, add the bacon and cook for 7–8 minutes, stirring frequently, until crisp and golden. Remove with a slotted spoon and drain on kitchen paper. Add the chestnuts to the pan and sauté in the bacon fat for several minutes, stirring frequently, until lightly golden. Transfer to a bowl and add the bacon.

Ten minutes before eating, melt the butter in a large frying pan over a medium-high heat, add the sprouts, season and sauté for 7–8 minutes until lightly golden. Add the bacon and chestnuts just before the end to heat through.

This purée plays on the deliciously aromatic flavour of Brussels sprouts, and with a bit of luck even those who normally decline could be tempted, not least because they probably won't recognise what it is unless you tell them.

brussels sprout and parsley purée

900g Brussels sprouts, base
   trimmed and outer leaves discarded
2 scant teaspoons red wine vinegar
150g crème fraîche
4 tablespoons coarsely chopped
   fresh flat-leaf parsley
sea salt, black pepper
a knob of salted butter

Serves 6

Bring a large pan of salted water to the boil, add the sprouts and simmer for 15–20 minutes, until very tender. Drain them in a colander and leave for a minute or two to steam dry. Place them in the bowl of a food processor with the vinegar, crème fraîche, parsley and some seasoning and whiz to a smooth purée. Return the purée to the saucepan and gently reheat when required. Drop a knob of butter into the centre and serve.

If you know you have a house full of sprout-haters, and even a buttery purée is unlikely to pass muster, this is a fine alternative. It's great with any roast or pie. You could add some nibs of chestnut too, and the bacon is optional.

green bean medley with crispy bacon

150ml white wine

3 shallots, peeled and finely chopped

75g unsalted butter, diced

400g fine green beans, stalk
  ends trimmed

400g sugar snaps, stalk ends trimmed

150g rindless unsmoked streaky
  bacon, diced

Serves 6

To make the sauce, place the wine and shallots in a small saucepan, bring to the boil and reduce to a couple of tablespoons, then whisk in the butter.

At the same time, bring a large pan of salted water to the boil. Cook the beans for 4–5 minutes, adding the sugar snaps 1 minute before the end, then drain them into a colander.

Meanwhile put the bacon into a large frying pan over a medium heat, and fry in the rendered fat for 7–9 minutes until golden and crisp, stirring frequently. Drain on kitchen paper.

Toss the vegetables with the sauce, and mix in the bacon. You can also cook everything in advance, reheat the vegetables in the sauce, then add the bacon.

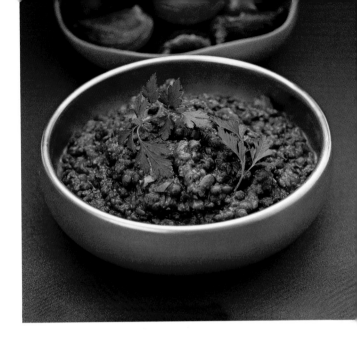

Savoury lentils go down a treat with roast ham. I also always dish them up with *petit salé*, thick slices of poached belly bacon that we grill over an open fire. If you add a little more stock, and any tasty ends of ham or turkey, you have the makings of a hearty soup. The recipe is a basic – add any veggies you have to hand.

creamy lentils

25g unsalted butter

2 slim carrots, peeled and thinly sliced

3 sticks of celery heart, trimmed
   and thinly sliced

5 garlic cloves, peeled and
   halved lengthways

300g French or Le Puy green lentils

1 litre vegetable or chicken stock

a pinch of dried chilli flakes

1 bay leaf

sea salt

coarsely chopped fresh flat-leaf parsley
   to serve (optional)

Serves 6

Melt the butter in a medium-size saucepan over a medium heat. Add the carrot and celery and fry for 6–7 minutes until softened and starting to colour, stirring occasionally, adding the garlic shortly before the end. Add the lentils and fry for a minute or two longer, stirring, then add the stock, chilli and bay leaf. Bring to the boil, cover and simmer for 25–40 minutes, until tender.

Discarding the bay leaf, put a few ladles of the lentils containing plenty of juices into a liquidiser and blend. Stir this back into the lentils, and season with salt. This part isn't essential, however. The lentils should be quite soupy at this point, so add a little more stock if necessary. You can also reheat them, in which case again you might need to add a little more stock. Serve scattered with parsley if wished.

If you can't face juggling three different veg, then this is the one for you – potatoes, parsnips and sprouts roasted as one. A little honey drizzled over towards the end ensures the veg arrive on the plate particularly sticky and caramelised.

all-in-one honey roast veg

800g maincrop potatoes, peeled
    and cut into 3–4cm pieces
600g parsnips, trimmed and peeled,
    halved or quartered lengthways
    where thick and cut into
    2 shorter lengths
100g unsalted butter, melted
sea salt, black pepper
600g Brussels sprouts, base trimmed
    and outer leaves discarded
2 tablespoons runny honey

Serves 6

Preheat the oven to 180°C fan/200°C/gas mark 6. Bring two medium-size pans of salted water to the boil. Add the potatoes to one and the parsnips to the other and cook for 5 minutes. Drain them into different sieves, and set aside for a few minutes for the surface moisture to evaporate. Return the potatoes to the pan and give them a shake, add a third of the butter and some seasoning and toss to coat them, then tip into a large roasting dish and cook for 10 minutes. Toss the parsnips with another third of the butter and some seasoning, then add to the potatoes in the roasting dish and cook for a further 45 minutes.

In the meantime, bring a medium-size pan of salted water to the boil. Add the sprouts and cook for 8 minutes, then drain them into a sieve and leave for a few minutes. Toss in the pan with the remaining butter and some seasoning.

Turn the temperature up to 200°C fan/220°C/gas mark 7 (i.e. on removing the turkey from the oven), mix the sprouts into the potatoes and parsnips, drizzle over the honey and cook for another 15–20 minutes until golden and caramelised.

The honey-mustard glaze here ensures that these bacon rolls emerge from the oven gorgeously sticky and golden. They also go down very well as cocktail eats if you are hunting for popular ideas, in which case make them small, using cocktail sausages.

honey-mustard chipolata rolls

12 chipolatas (350–400g)

groundnut or vegetable oil (optional)

12 rashers of pancetta or rindless
   streaky bacon

1 tablespoon set honey

1 tablespoon Dijon mustard

Serves 6–12

Preheat the oven to 180°C fan/200°C/gas mark 6. Heat a large non-stick frying pan over a medium-high heat and colour the sausages all over for 5–7 minutes, adding a drop of oil to the pan if necessary. Wind a rasher of pancetta or bacon along the length of each sausage – you may like to secure them with a cocktail stick. Arrange the rolls, spaced slightly apart, in a roasting dish and roast for 20 minutes. In the meantime, blend the honey and mustard in a small bowl. Generously brush the sausages with the honey-mustard glaze on both sides and cook for another 15 minutes, until golden and sticky.

I prefer to slip out the insides of some good sausages rather than use sausage meat, as they are always that much better flavoured.

sage, chestnut and apple sausage meat balls

25g unsalted butter

1 onion, peeled and finely chopped

1 apple, peeled, cored and
  finely diced

2 tablespoons fresh sage leaves,
  finely sliced

150g cooked and peeled
  chestnuts, sliced

sea salt, black pepper

700g sausages

Serves 6

Melt the butter in a large frying pan over a medium heat, add the onion, apple and sage, and fry for 5–6 minutes, until softened and glossy, without colouring. Add the chestnuts, season and cook for a minute or two longer, then leave to cool.

Slit the sausages open and slip the meat into a large bowl. Add the chestnut mixture and combine. Take heaped tablespoons of the mixture and shape into balls. Cover and chill until required.

Preheat the oven to 180°C fan/200°C/gas mark 6. Arrange the stuffing balls spaced a little way apart in a roasting dish and bake for 20 minutes. Turn the oven up to 200°C fan/220°C/gas mark 7 (i.e. on removing the turkey from the oven) and cook the balls for another 25 minutes or until they are golden.

On the Continent the ultimate stuffings are made with foie gras, and this luxurious little forcemeat that we can eat with a clear conscience is not dissimilar. It's also the cheat of the equation, a ten-minuter if that. Any pâté can be used; my first choice would be either a *pâté forestière*, with little snippets of mushroom, or a smooth pâté laced with apple. But there are any number of gorgeous Christmas takes around.

faux foie gras stuffing

400g pâté, diced

finely grated zest of 1 lemon

4 tablespoons coarsely chopped
   fresh flat-leaf parsley

1 tablespoon Madeira or Marsala

100g fresh white breadcrumbs

25g unsalted butter

Serves 6
Makes enough stuffing
for 1 x 5kg turkey

Combine the pâté, lemon zest, parsley, Madeira or Marsala and half the breadcrumbs in a bowl and stuff the turkey.

Up to an hour before eating, melt the butter in a large frying pan over a medium heat. Once it is sizzling nicely, fry the remaining breadcrumbs until golden, stirring constantly, then transfer them to a bowl.

Spoon the stuffing out of the bird after carving, and serve scattered with the breadcrumbs.

A classic sage and onion stuffing has to be one of my favourite ways of filling the bird, and takes me back to Christmas Eve in my mother's kitchen, when she mixed it up in a large mixing bowl, covered it with a tea towel and it wafted the gentle scent of sage all afternoon and evening. It soaks up all the turkey juices from within as it cooks, and it's simple.

sage and onion stuffing

50g unsalted butter

2 large onions, peeled, quartered
   and thinly sliced

1 tablespoon finely sliced fresh
   sage leaves

finely grated zest of 1 lemon, plus a
   squeeze of lemon juice

100g fresh white breadcrumbs

sea salt, black pepper

Serves 6
Makes enough stuffing
for 1 x 5kg turkey

Melt half the butter in a large frying pan over a medium heat, add the onions and cook gently for 10–15 minutes, until lightly golden and caramelised, stirring frequently. Stir in the sage just before the end, then remove from the heat and add the lemon zest, a generous squeeze of lemon juice and the remaining butter. Once this has melted add the breadcrumbs and season with salt and pepper.

in or out of the bird

The notion that stuffing the turkey is in some way dangerous is one of those myths. Provided you observe a few guidelines it is perfectly safe. That said, I always cook sausage meat stuffings outside the bird, but only because that caramelised golden exterior is too good to pass up, and 'sausage balls' (for want of a more poetic description) are tantalisingly delicious.

Fill the main cavity of the turkey with the stuffing, packing it loosely, and leaving half the cavity empty but plugging the opening. This will allow the air to circulate inside the bird, in effect creating a mini oven. You can also stuff the neck end, using a different stuffing if you like or half an onion with a couple of sprigs of thyme or rosemary and a piece of lemon zest.

This lovely torte was born of a determination that there had to be a better way with nut roasts. So here we have the luxury of toasted almonds and cashews, with the succulence of spinach and molten goat's cheese, in a recipe that doubles as a vegetarian main course or soignée stuffing cooked alongside the bird. What more could you ask?

homage to nut roast

900g spinach
100g flaked almonds
100g roasted cashews, chopped
finely grated zest of 1 lemon
2 teaspoons fresh thyme leaves
sea salt, black pepper
3 tablespoons extra virgin olive oil
    or melted unsalted butter
4 tablespoons fresh white breadcrumbs
200g medium-mature goat's cheese,
    rind discarded, sliced

Serves 6–8

Bring a large pan of salted water to the boil, add the spinach, bring back to the boil and cook for 2 minutes, then drain into a colander and leave to cool.

At the same time preheat the oven to 180°C fan/200°C/gas mark 6, spread the almonds in a thin layer in a roasting dish or baking tray and toast for 9–10 minutes until lightly golden.

Press out as much water as you can from the spinach using your hands, then slice or chop it. Place it in a large bowl, add the chopped cashews, flaked almonds, lemon zest, thyme, some seasoning and a couple of tablespoons of olive oil or butter, and combine.

Toss the breadcrumbs with the remaining tablespoon of oil or butter and scatter half of them over the base of a 20cm cake tin at least 4cm deep with a removable base. Press half the spinach mixture on top, then lay over the goat's cheese and repeat with the remaining spinach. Scatter with the rest of the breadcrumbs. You can prepare the torte to this point in advance, in which case cover and chill it.

Preheat the oven to 180°C fan/200°C/gas mark 6 and cook the torte for 35–40 minutes, until golden and crisp on the surface. Serve cut in wedges.

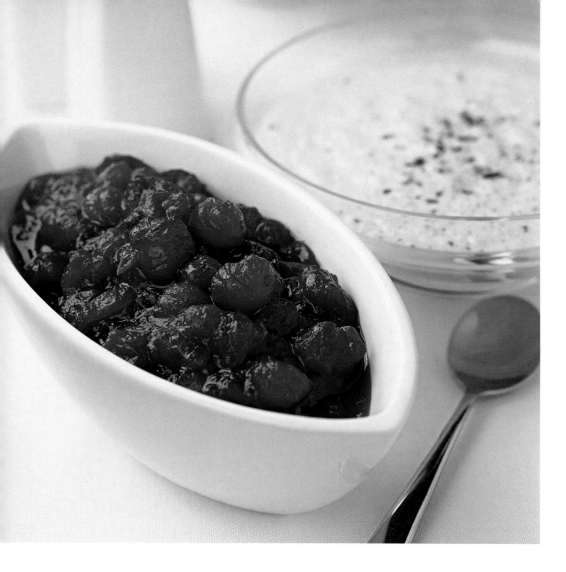

Turkey is unimaginable without this sweet and sour condiment. Just one tip: cooking the cranberries before adding the sugar avoids tough skins. That aside, I don't think it's improved by the addition of spices or more alcohol – keep it simple.

cranberry sauce

450g cranberries
juice of 2 oranges
125g caster sugar

Serves 6

Place the cranberries and orange juice in a small saucepan, bring to the boil, cover and simmer over a low heat for 5 minutes. Stir in the sugar, turn the heat up to medium and simmer uncovered for another 10–15 minutes, until the juices are reduced and syrupy. Transfer the sauce to a bowl, cover with clingfilm and leave to cool.

This sauce can be prepared several days in advance, in which case chill and bring it back up to room temperature before serving.

That sweet savour of onion and the hint of bay and cloves are what a bread sauce is all about, hence this version, which is a departure from the norm. Basically you make a creamy onion purée and combine it with a bread sauce base. It has the advantage that you can make it an hour or two ahead and then very gently rewarm it. I can't be alone in having a penchant for cold turkey and bread sauce sandwiches, so this is another one to cook plenty of, bearing in mind the days to come.

bread sauce

30g unsalted butter

1 large onion (ideally white), peeled, halved and sliced

¾ teaspoon sea salt

100ml double cream

1 bay leaf

5 cloves

75g fresh white breadcrumbs

300ml full-cream milk

freshly grated nutmeg

Serves 6

Melt the butter in a small non-stick saucepan over a medium heat. Add the onion, sprinkle over the salt and cook gently for 6–8 minutes, stirring frequently, until soft and silky but not coloured. Add the cream, bay leaf and cloves, cover, and cook over the lowest heat for about 5 minutes, stirring at least once. Remove from the heat and leave to infuse for 20 minutes. Discard the bay leaf and cloves and whiz to a smooth purée in a food processor.

Combine the breadcrumbs and milk in the same non-stick saucepan, and bring to the boil, stirring until smooth. Simmer for 7–10 minutes over a low heat, stirring occasionally, until you have a thick sauce. Add the onion purée and heat through, and season with freshly grated nutmeg and a little more salt if needed. Unlike a normal bread sauce, this can be made in advance, anything up to a couple of hours. Cover the surface with clingfilm and leave in the pan on the hob. Gently reheat to serve.

making breadcrumbs

Remove the crusts from some day-old coarse-textured white bread, break it up into chunks and whiz in a food processor until reduced to fine crumbs. Should you have forgotten to buy the bread a day ahead you can use fresh bread, provided it is a good-quality pain de campagne or other such rustic bread with a sturdy, dry crumb.

This is my basic gravy to go with the turkey. It make about 500ml, but if you want even more, simply step up the ingredients accordingly, or you could make the extra gravy below.

gorgeous gravy

100ml port
1 tablespoon plain flour
500ml giblet stock (see page 104)
    or chicken stock
sea salt, black pepper

Serves 6–8

Skim off any excess fat from the roasting tray leaving just 1 or 2 tablespoons. Place the roasting tray on a lowish heat, add the port and cook for several minutes until reduced by half, scraping up all the sticky roasting juices in the bottom of the tray. Stir in the flour and once this is seething, gradually stir in the stock. Simmer the gravy long and hard enough for it to amalgamate into a smooth sauce. Taste and season if necessary. Add any juices given out on carving the turkey and pour into a jug to serve. If there are a lot of bits you may like to strain it first.

This is for whenever you want MORE gravy, without recourse to artificial powders. You could add a little Madeira or medium sherry in lieu of red wine for an even richer flavour.

extra gravy

2 tablespoons vegetable oil
500g mixture of diced onion,
    celery, carrot and leek
2 garlic cloves, peeled and
    finely chopped
1 tablespoon plain flour
150ml red wine
500ml giblet stock (see page 104)
    or chicken stock
sea salt, black pepper

Serves 6–8

Heat the oil in a large saucepan over a medium heat, then add the vegetables and fry for 30–35 minutes, stirring occasionally, until really well coloured, almost black (this is your gravy browning). Add the garlic a few minutes before the end. Sprinkle over the flour and stir, and then gradually add the red wine and cook for a couple of minutes, when it will thicken. Stir in the stock in two or three goes, add some seasoning, and simmer for about 5 minutes. Pass the gravy through a sieve, pressing out as much as possible from the vegetables. If it tastes at all thin, you can simmer it a few minutes longer, and check the seasoning. If you let it stand for any length of time, then there may be a little oil on the surface, which you can skim off. Add any juices given out on slicing the roast.

A rich, creamy gravy that makes a luxurious touch with Christmas dinner. The sweet wine can be varied; skim off a little of whatever you have bought in to drink.

sauternes gravy

½ teaspoon Dijon mustard
100ml Sauternes
1 tablespoon plain flour
300ml giblet or chicken stock
100ml double cream
sea salt, black pepper

Serves 6–8

Skim off any excess fat from the roasting tray, leaving just 1 or 2 tablespoons. Place the roasting tray on a lowish heat, stir in the mustard, then the Sauternes, and cook for several minutes until reduced by half, scraping up all the sticky roasting juices in the bottom of the tray. Stir in the flour and once this is seething, gradually stir in the stock and the cream. Simmer the gravy until you have a smooth sauce, and season to taste – the Sauternes welcomes a generous pinch or two of salt. Add any juices given out on carving the turkey and strain into a jug or sauceboat to serve.

giblet stock

turkey or goose gizzard, neck bone
    and heart
1 tablespoon goose fat or
    groundnut oil
sea salt, black pepper
500–700ml water or chicken stock

Serves 6–8
Makes 500–700ml

Preheat the oven to 200°C fan/220°C/gas mark 7. If buying your bird from a friendly butchers, you could prevail upon them to chop up the gizzard and neck bone for you. Otherwise, chop the heart and place it together with the whole gizzard and neck bone in a small roasting dish. Drizzle over a tablespoon of goose fat or groundnut oil, season with salt and pepper and roast for 20 minutes until lightly coloured. Place the giblets in a small saucepan with the water or chicken stock, (keeping hold of the roasting dish if you're making gravy for the roast goose with prune and apple stuffing on page 54). Bring to a simmer, skim the surface if necessary, cover and simmer over a very low heat for 30–45 minutes, then strain.

lovely leftovers

Where do we begin? Boxing Day brings with it a culture in eating all of its own, that's as ad hoc as a game of charades. When hunger strikes it's each to their own whim, my own being those heartstoppingly good bread sauce and turkey sandwiches. When no one's looking, that is, just as few would care to admit to mulled wine trifle for breakfast, and other such outlandish snacking.

Writ large in all the cooking we do for Christmas is providing the leftovers that will feed us in their own sweet tradition in the days between Christmas and New Year. Turkey should always be ordered a size larger than you are likely to want on the day for the dividend thereafter, all that succulent dark meat that clings to the bones but evaded carving, and the gorgeous brown stock that results from the carcass. No other potful matches it at any other stage of the year. It is the foundation for soups galore, and for the must-eat turkey and ham pie. Which leads us to the other great roast to enjoy in excess, ham. Its poaching liquor makes for fab lentil soups, and any leftover snippets will be lauded in all manner of salads, pies and toasties.

Cold leftover veggies make a fine frying-pan hash, nicely peppered up with chilli. Even the leftover stuffing can be put to good use, with some salad leaves and a lightly poached egg, as a kind of inside-out Scotch egg. While leftover Christmas pud or cake will lend themselves to a divine bread-and-butter-style pud in lieu of the panettone on page 137.

Sweet, thick and mealy, and full of the scent of Christmas. You want a good old-fashioned banger here for the crispy sausage nibs – a Cumberland is ideal – though beware wandering fingers if they're sitting around for any length of time.

chestnut and madeira soup with crispy sausage

50g unsalted butter

1 onion, peeled and chopped

1 celery heart, trimmed and sliced

2 carrots, trimmed, peeled and sliced

1 parsnip, trimmed, peeled and sliced

500g cooked and peeled chestnuts

150ml Madeira

1.2 litres turkey or other poultry stock

sea salt, black pepper

1 tablespoon groundnut or
    vegetable oil

3 Cumberland sausages
    (approx. 200g), skinned

coarsely chopped fresh flat-leaf
    parsley to serve

Serves 6

Melt the butter in a large saucepan over a medium heat, add the onion, celery, carrots and parsnip, and fry for about 10 minutes, stirring frequently, until softened and lightly golden. Add the chestnuts and cook for a minute or two longer, then add the Madeira and simmer until well reduced. Pour in the stock, add some seasoning, bring to the boil and simmer for 15 minutes, until the vegetables are tender. Purée the soup in a liquidiser, then return it to the saucepan and taste for seasoning.

Heat the oil in a large non-stick frying pan over a medium heat. Roughly slice and add the sausage meat, and fry for 6–9 minutes until golden and caramelised, breaking it up into little nibs with a metal spatula as it firms up, so you end up with lots of little crispy bits. Drain it on a double thickness of kitchen paper. Serve the hot soup with some of the crispy sausage in the centre, and some chopped parsley.

If you have an eye to this as the main course, then I would make two or three times the amount of Stilton toasts, as they disappear with or without the soup. In fact they make very good hand-me-rounds too.

celeriac and apple soup

Soup

75g unsalted butter

2 onions, peeled and
   chopped

2 leeks, trimmed and sliced

2 carrots, trimmed, peeled
   and diced

1 celery heart, trimmed
   and sliced

1 celeriac bulb (approx.
   900g), peeled and diced

1 apple, peeled, cored
   and diced

200ml dry cider

1.2 litres turkey or other
   poultry or vegetable stock

sea salt, black pepper

Toasts

6 thin slices of baguette

unsalted butter

60g Stilton, crumbled

Serves 6

Melt the butter in a large saucepan over a medium-low heat. Add the onions, leeks, carrots and celery and cook gently for 10–12 minutes, until glossy and starting to colour, stirring occasionally. Add the celeriac and apple and cook for about 5 minutes longer. Pour in the cider and cook until well reduced, then add the stock and some seasoning, bring to the boil and simmer for 20 minutes, until the celeriac is tender. Purée the soup in a liquidiser in batches and press it through a sieve, then adjust the seasoning.

To make the Stilton toasts, heat the grill and toast the baguette slices on both sides. Spread with butter, crumble over the Stilton and return to the grill until melted and sizzling. Reheat the soup if necessary, ladle into bowls and float the toasts in the soup.

Buy in lots of these roots before Christmas; they'll keep well in the veggie basket and make for a fabulously aromatic thick sweet soup that's given a savoury edge by a rich turkey stock.

parsnip and rosemary soup

Soup

50g unsalted butter

2 onions, peeled and chopped

1 leek, trimmed and sliced

4 sticks of celery heart, trimmed
   and sliced

2 garlic cloves, peeled and finely chopped

600g parsnips, trimmed, peeled,
   halved and sliced

4 x 10cm sprigs of fresh rosemary

juice of ½ lemon

1 litre turkey or other poultry
   or vegetable stock

sea salt, black pepper

150ml whipping cream

Bits

250g rindless smoked streaky
   bacon, diced

40g pine nuts

Serves 6

Melt the butter in a large saucepan over a medium-low heat. Add the onions, leek, celery and garlic and cook gently for 15–20 minutes, until softened and glossy, stirring occasionally. Add the parsnips, rosemary and lemon juice and cook for another 15 minutes, again stirring occasionally. Add the stock and some seasoning, bring to the boil and simmer for 10 minutes. Remove the rosemary sprigs and liquidise the soup; you may need to do this in batches. Stir in the cream and taste for seasoning.

Shortly before serving, put the bacon in a large frying pan over a medium heat and fry in the rendered fat until golden and crisp, stirring frequently. Transfer it to a double layer of kitchen paper to drain. Now fry the pine nuts in the bacon fat until golden, stirring almost constantly, and drain these on kitchen paper as well. Once cool, combine the bacon and nuts in a bowl and serve scattered over the hot soup.

Butternut squash and scallops go together a treat, but the soup will be just as good on its own, or with a little Stilton or some snippets of ham. The stock is all-important here, and needs to be that little bit stronger than usual.

butternut squash soup with saffron cream

Soup
50g unsalted butter

1 large onion, peeled
and chopped

1 celery heart, trimmed
and sliced

2 leeks, trimmed and sliced

3 garlic cloves, peeled and
finely chopped

2kg butternut squash, skin
and seeds removed, cut
into chunks

800ml strong turkey or other
poultry stock

sea salt, white pepper

juice of ½ lemon

Saffron Cream
approx. 20 saffron filaments,
ground and blended with
1 teaspoon boiling water

100g crème fraîche

Scallops
12 plump scallops

1 tablespoon extra virgin
olive oil

a squeeze of lemon juice

coarsely chopped fresh
flat-leaf parsley

Serves 6

Melt the butter in a large saucepan over a medium heat. Add the onion, celery and leeks and cook gently for about 10 minutes, until glossy, softened and just starting to colour. Stir occasionally and add the garlic shortly before the end. Add the squash and cook for a few minutes longer, stirring now and again, then add the stock and press the vegetables down – they may not be completely covered. Season with plenty of salt and a little pepper, bring to the boil, cover and simmer for 15 minutes. Purée the soup in batches in a liquidiser, then stir in the lemon juice and taste for seasoning. You should have a thick, silky orange soup.

Blend the saffron infusion with the crème fraîche and a little salt in a bowl. To prepare the scallops, pull the corals away from the white meat, removing the surrounding girdle and the white gristle at the same time. Cut off and reserve the corals and slice the meat into discs. Toss these in a bowl with the olive oil and some seasoning. Heat a large non-stick frying pan over a high heat, and briefly sear about a third of the scallops at a time until lightly caramelised, about 30 seconds each side. Once they are all cooked squeeze over a little lemon juice. Serve the hot soup with a little of the saffron cream spooned over, some of the scallops and a sprinkling of parsley.

Something warming and spicy for the post-Christmas chill, usually made with chicken, but turkey does just as nicely. Don't be put off by the lengthy list of ingredients – its charm is its complexity and it's comparatively quick to muster.

turkey mulligatawny

25g unsalted butter

2 leeks, trimmed and thinly sliced

2 sticks of celery, trimmed
   and thinly sliced

2 medium carrots or 1 large,
   trimmed, peeled, halved and sliced

2 teaspoons finely grated fresh ginger

1 medium-hot fresh red chilli,
   deseeded and finely diced

1 teaspoon turmeric

½ teaspoon ground cumin

½ teaspoon ground coriander

225g maincrop potatoes, peeled
   and cut into 1cm dice

1 bay leaf

1.2 litres turkey stock

sea salt

50g basmati rice

200ml coconut milk

150g cooked turkey, cut into
   fine strips

2 tablespoons lemon juice

coarsely chopped fresh coriander
   to serve

Serves 6

Melt the butter in a large saucepan over a medium heat, add the leeks, celery, carrots, ginger and chilli and fry for about 5 minutes until softened, stirring frequently. Stir in the spices and then the potato, and add the bay leaf. Pour in the stock and season with salt, then bring to the boil and simmer over a low heat for 10 minutes. Stir in the rice and cook for another 10–15 minutes, until it is tender.

At the end of cooking, add the coconut milk, the turkey and the lemon juice and taste for seasoning. Reheat the soup almost to boiling point. You can either serve the mulligatawny as it is, or briefly whiz it in a food processor to a thick textured soup, first removing the bay leaf. Serve in warm bowls, scattered with coriander.

For those who find Stilton a little too assertive, I would opt for a big wedge of Wensleydale on the sideboard. It's a really elegant cheese, sharp and buttery and just the ticket with after-dinner dates.

chicory, wensleydale, hazelnut and date salad

Salad
50g skinned hazelnuts
4 heads of chicory, base trimmed
75g lamb's lettuce
6 medjool dates, quartered lengthways
150g Wensleydale, cut into 1cm dice

Serves 6

Dressing
1 tablespoon red wine vinegar
1 teaspoon Dijon mustard
½ teaspoon caster sugar
sea salt, black pepper
4 tablespoons hazelnut oil
4 tablespoons groundnut oil

Preheat the oven to 180°C fan/200°C/gas mark 6. Scatter the nuts over the base of a small baking dish and toast for 9–10 minutes, until golden. Leave to cool, then halve or coarsely chop them.

To make the dressing, whisk the vinegar with a tablespoon of water, the mustard, sugar and some seasoning, then whisk in the oils until amalgamated. Discarding the outer chicory leaves if they are damaged, finely slice the heads lengthways. Combine the leaves, dates and hazelnuts in a large salad bowl. The salad can be prepared to this point up to an hour in advance, in which case cover and set aside in a cool place.

To serve, give the dressing a whisk, pour over and toss, then gently mix in the cheese.

Chantenay carrots are small and plump with a lovely flavour and texture. There is no need to peel them, and they look particularly good in a salad. This one's great with sliced roast ham.

roast carrot and parsnip salad with crunchy seeds

25g sunflower seeds

25g pumpkin seeds

15g sesame seeds

5 tablespoons extra virgin olive oil

500g Chantenay carrots

sea salt, black pepper

500g parsnips, trimmed, peeled and cut into batons

2 tablespoons white wine vinegar

1 teaspoon runny honey

100ml fresh smooth orange juice

50g rocket or lamb's lettuce

Serves 6–8

Preheat the oven to 180°C fan/200°C/gas mark 6. Scatter the seeds over the base of a baking dish and toast for 9–10 minutes, then leave to cool.

Heat a tablespoon of oil in a large frying pan over a highish heat. Add the carrots and some seasoning and fry for 4–8 minutes, stirring occasionally, until coloured. Tip them into a roasting dish, and colour the parsnips in the same way, adding another tablespoon of oil to the pan (these will colour a little quicker). Blend the vinegar with the honey in a bowl, then stir in the orange juice and pour over the carrots and parsnips. Roast for 25 minutes, by which time the liquid should have evaporated and the vegetables be tender. Pour over another 3 tablespoons of oil, scatter over some more sea salt and leave to cool.

Scatter the seeds over the veg, then gently mix in the salad leaves and transfer to a serving bowl.

So just what do you do with all that leftover stuffing? It was after eating a Scotch egg at the French-inspired restaurant La Trompette in Chiswick, West London, that I dreamt up this deconstructed version in the hope of revisiting it. Theirs was a soft runny yolk within a sausage meat casing that spilled as you cut into it. This cannot claim any such technical greatness, but is a friendly plate of grub all the same.

inside-out scotch egg

400g leftover stuffing
   (ideally a sausage one)
a mixture of rocket leaves, sprigs
   of fresh coriander, dill and parsley,
   to serve 4
white wine vinegar
4 large organic eggs
groundnut oil
lemon juice
sea salt

Serves 4

Fill your largest saucepan with water and bring it to the boil. Slice the stuffing and arrange it on four large plates. Place the salad leaves in a large bowl. Add a good slug of white wine vinegar to the boiling water. Now turn the heat down and keep the water at a trembling simmer while the eggs are poaching.

Break the eggs one at a time into a teacup (or use four teacups). Gently stir the water into a whirlpool using a large spoon and drop the eggs into it. They will immediately sink to the bottom of the pan, leaving strands of white floating. After about 4 minutes, remove them using a slotted spoon, trimming off the tendrils of white against the side of the saucepan.

Place the poached eggs on top of the stuffing. Toss the leaves with just enough oil to coat them, a few drops of lemon juice and a pinch of sea salt and divide between the plates. Serve straight away.

A big plate of hash peppered with Lea & Perrins is essential to the post-Christmas proceedings, and you can include any leftover veg as well as cooking them from scratch as suggested. A large frying pan will do for two to three, so if you are more than this, double the quantities and use two pans.

ham and root veg hash

200g carrots, trimmed,
    peeled and diced
200g swede, peeled and diced
200g parsnips, trimmed,
    peeled and diced
3 tablespoons extra virgin olive oil
1 red onion, peeled, halved and sliced
2 sprigs of fresh rosemary
3 medium-hot red chillies
4 garlic cloves, peeled
sea salt
3 slices of roast ham,
    cut into broad strips

Serves 2–3

Place the carrot, swede and parsnip in the top half of a steamer set over about 2cm of simmering water in the lower half and steam for 15 minutes. At the same time heat the olive oil in a large frying pan over a medium-low heat and gently cook the onion for 12–15 minutes, stirring frequently, until nicely golden and slightly crisp. Remove to a bowl and reserve.

Add the steamed vegetables to the frying pan with the rosemary, chillies and garlic cloves and sauté, again over a medium-low heat, for about 25 minutes, turning them frequently. Season with salt halfway through. At the end of cooking add the onions and ham to heat through. Discard the rosemary and garlic cloves and serve. The flesh of the chillies can be eaten, scraped off the skin.

This Coronation turkey has nothing in common with the usual bottled mayo flavoured with ready-made curry powder, and will hopefully silence any sceptical critics. Use it to fill sandwiches or serve it with a rice salad, scattering over some toasted flaked almonds or pine nuts, and some chopped coriander. Don't be put off by the long list of ingredients, it's all said and done in 30 minutes. You could also use chicken.

coronation turkey with apricots

2 tomatoes
1/3 teaspoon ground cumin
1/3 teaspoon ground coriander
1/4 teaspoon turmeric
1/8 teaspoon cayenne pepper
1/4 teaspoon ground cinnamon
1/4 teaspoon ground ginger
225ml groundnut oil, plus
    2 tablespoons
1 onion, peeled, halved and
    thinly sliced
75g ready-to-eat dried apricots,
    boiled for 10 minutes, sliced
sea salt
1 medium organic egg yolk
1 teaspoon Dijon mustard
a squeeze of lemon juice
black pepper
450g cooked turkey meat,
    cut into strips
cress to serve

Serves 4

Bring a small pan of water to the boil. Cut out a cone from the top of each tomato, dunk them into the boiling water for 20 seconds and then into cold water. Remove them, slip off the skins and coarsely chop them. Combine all the spices in a bowl.

Heat the 2 tablespoons of oil in a large frying pan over a medium-low heat, add the onion and sauté for several minutes, until soft and translucent. Add the spices and give them a stir, then add the tomatoes and apricots and season with salt. Turn the heat down low and cook for 8–12 minutes, until the sauce is thick and reduced and the oil separates out from the tomatoes, stirring frequently. Transfer the mixture to a bowl or plate and leave to cool.

Whisk the egg yolk with the mustard in a bowl, then slowly whisk in the groundnut oil, just a few drops at a time to begin with. Combine the mayonnaise with the cooled tomato and onion mixture, add a squeeze of lemon juice and a grinding of black pepper. Stir in the turkey, sprinkle over the mustard and cress and taste for salt.

christmas puddings

You don't even have to like Christmas pudding to be filled with contented pleasure at that moment after a big Christmas dinner, when the lights are turned out and the Christmas pudding lit with a halo of blue flame is ceremoniously carried in. It is one of the great rituals of the festivities. And most of us manage just a small spoonful of this incredibly rich pudding. A succulent mass of dried fruits and spices, fused with molten suet and infused with brandy, every time I make one I find it a matter of wonder that this loose mixture can turn into the dark sophisticated pudding that it does simply with many hours steaming.

My mother always used to serve it with a lily-white rum custard as well as brandy butter, which is every bit as delectable as bread sauce with turkey. This is the pudding recipe I grew up with, and the only short cut I have taken is with the suet, which my mother used to grate by hand. She always made it well in advance of Christmas, so it is one to get mixing on 'Stir-up Sunday', or at least in time for it to mature. Should you be looking for something even lighter than that, with just a little in the way of dried fruit and booze to set the tone, then a panettone pudding is probably the one for you, a Christmassy bread and butter pud.

Next on the list is something with chestnuts. The bûche de Noël on page 166 will stand in for a Christmas pudding, and the little mont blancs in a glass are heavenly eaten with meringues. I love a trifle on Boxing Day – it seems the perfect pud to wheel out after the ham, soothing layer upon layer of jelly and sponge, custard and syllabub, and this of course can be made a couple of days in advance, to its credit. While by contrast a wobbly red cranberry jelly not only sings with goodness but makes an ethereal end to any rich meal. My family love this white Christmas version of a cheesecake, as well as the chocolatey 'tira-mi-su' torte.

my grandmother's christmas pudding

This is the Christmas pud I grew up with; it's really dark, rich and moist, a recipe my mother thinks she was given by my paternal grandmother. It's on a well-stained page in her handwritten book of recipes, in faded ink, with no instructions at all, simply a list of ingredients, but she's filled me in with the rest. She used to mature these puds one year for the next, on the top shelf of a cupboard in my bedroom, and the lingering scent that escaped every time it was opened lies deep in my memory. To be on the safe side, though, if maturing it for a year I prefer the fridge.

Traditionally it should be made on 'Stir-up Sunday', the weekend before Advent, four Sundays away from Christmas. The 'stir-up' actually has nothing to do with making the pudding itself; rather it is taken from the collect for the day in the Church of England's Book of Common Prayer, read after the communion:

'Stir-up, we beseech thee, O Lord, the wills of thy faithful people;
That they, plenteously bringing forth the fruit of good works, may of thee
be plenteously rewarded; through Jesus Christ our Lord.'

So returning from church to your kitchen, ravenous, you take it in turns with the rest of the family to give the pudding mixture a stir, east to west in honour of the Three Wise Men, and to make a silent wish. You include a coin at your own risk, you could also include a ring, as a symbol of marriage, and a thimble brings good luck.

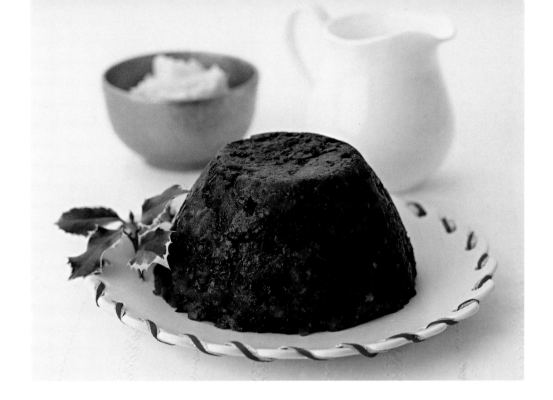

225g seedless raisins

125g currants

125g sultanas

1 glass of brandy (approx. 100ml),
  plus extra to flambé

125g demerara sugar

225g shredded beef suet

225g white breadcrumbs

50g crème de riz or ground rice

½ teaspoon ground ginger

½ teaspoon ground cinnamon

½ teaspoon ground nutmeg

½ teaspoon sea salt

2 apples, peeled, cored and diced

50g chopped mixed peel

15g chopped almonds

2 medium eggs, beaten

2 tablespoons full cream milk

holly to decorate

Each pud serves 6–8
Makes 2

Mix the dried fruits in a large mixing bowl and pour over the brandy. Add all the remaining ingredients (except the holly), and take it in turns to stir the pudding from east to west while making your wish, taking care to mix it well. Butter two 16cm/900ml pudding basins (see page 9) and place a square of baking paper in the bottom of each one. Divide the mixture between them, pressing it well down – the pudding won't expand hugely, but there should be about 1cm of room at the top. Cover with a sheet of baking paper that comes about halfway down the sides, and tie it in place with string.

Cooking the puddings can be steamy stuff, and the best method is to either place them in one or two cast-iron casseroles with tightly fitting lids, or in a large saucepan, wrapping the lid in a clean tea-towel so the corners drape over the top. Fill the pans with water to half cover the pudding basins, bring to the boil, add the puds, cover and steam for 6 hours, topping up the water every 2 hours or so as necessary. Leave to cool completely in the pans, then remove the paper, re-cover and store in a cool dry place until Christmas.

On the day, steam for 2 hours as above to serve, then run a knife around the edge, place a plate on top and invert the pudding to turn it out. Stick with a sprig of holly and flambé with brandy.

This lily-white custard is heaven poured over Christmas pud, which needn't mean missing out on the brandy butter, have a little dab of that too. But it does need to be made to serve, so have everything at the ready and heat it just before eating. It's yummy served over hot mince pies (see page 150) as a pud too.

rum sauce

600ml full-cream milk
2 tablespoons cornflour
150ml double cream
2 tablespoons dark rum
75g white caster sugar

Serves 6–8

Blend a little of the milk with the cornflour in a small bowl. Add this to a small non-stick saucepan with the rest of the ingredients, bring to the boil, stirring as it thickens, and serve straight away.

The secret here is to whisk the butter until it is really light and fluffy, almost white.

brandy butter

175g unsalted butter, softened
175g icing sugar, sifted
5 tablespoons brandy or Armagnac

Serves 6–8

Whisk the butter in a bowl until it is really pale and mousse-like, using an electric whisk. Add the icing sugar and whisk again. Gradually beat in the brandy or Armagnac until you have a smooth creamy butter. Transfer to a bowl, cover and chill until required. Remove the butter from the fridge about 20 minutes before serving.

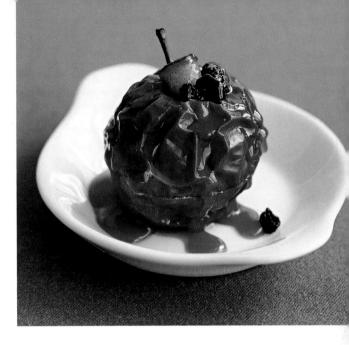

All the fun of the fair, these baked apples come bathed in a sparkling, rich caramel sauce. You could also jazz up the filling with a few spices, ground cinnamon, ginger and cloves.

baked toffee apples

25g unsalted butter, softened

25g light muscovado sugar

finely grated zest of 1 lemon,
   plus 1 tablespoon juice

40g raisins

30g currants

6 red eating apples

6 tablespoons golden syrup

1 tablespoon dark rum or water

crème fraîche to serve

Serves 6

Preheat the oven to 160°C fan/180°C/gas mark 4. Cream the butter and muscovado sugar together in a small bowl, then beat in the lemon zest and juice (don't worry if the mixture appears a little curdled at this point). Mix in the raisins and currants. Using the tip of a sharp knife, incise a circle around the middle of each apple. This ensures that as it cooks the apple has room to expand without the skin splitting. Now cut out the core. The easiest way to do this, unless you have an apple corer, is to remove a cone from the top and bottom of each one, and then trim the centre. If you try and slip out the whole centre from one end you can end up splitting the apple in two.

Loosely stuff the cavities with the dried fruit mixture to within 1cm of the top, and place the apples in a baking dish spaced slightly apart. Drizzle a tablespoon of syrup over each one and bake for 45 minutes, basting them every 15 minutes. Place the apples on plates, or transfer them to a serving dish and leave to cool for 10–15 minutes. Pour the syrup into a small saucepan, spooning any loose raisins and currants back inside the apples. Simmer until reduced by half and a deep caramel gold, then stir in a tablespoon of rum or water. Drizzle the caramel over the apples and serve with crème fraîche.

An old-fashioned trifle with sponges soaked in orange syrup, spread with strawberry jam and a fluffy syllabub on top, run through with a heady hit of almonds courtesy of the amaretti and amaretto. So nothing lavish then.

almond trifle

Base

4 oranges (medium-size rather
    than navel)
30g golden caster sugar
6 trifle sponges
120g strawberry jam
10 amaretti, plus a few more to serve
20g flaked almonds
icing sugar for dusting

Syllabub

finely grated zest of 1 orange,
    plus 2 tablespoons juice
a generous squeeze of lemon juice
120ml sweet sherry
2 tablespoons amaretto
40g icing sugar
300ml double cream

Serves 8

Halve and juice two of the oranges, and put into a small saucepan with the caster sugar over a medium heat. Simmer until reduced to 50ml of syrup. Arrange the trifle sponges on the base of a 20cm trifle dish at least 7cm deep, cutting them to fit and squeezing them in, and splash the syrup over. Place the jam in a bowl and work it with a spoon until it is smooth, then spread it over the sponges.

Slice the skin and outer pith off the remaining 2 oranges and run a small sharp knife between the segments to remove them from the pith that separates them. Drain the segments into a sieve set over a bowl, then scatter them over the trifle sponges. Arrange the ten amaretti on top.

To make the syllabub, whisk the orange zest and juice with the lemon juice, sherry, amaretto and icing sugar in a large bowl. Slowly whisk in the cream in a thin stream, and continue to whisk until you have a light and fluffy syllabub. While it needs to be the consistency of softly whipped cream, care should be taken not to overwhisk, otherwise it can separate. I use a hand-held electric whisk for this. Smooth the syllabub over the trifle base. Cover with clingfilm and chill overnight. During this time the syllabub will firm up, and the syrup and juices will continue to soak into the trifle sponges, which should be very moist by the time you serve it.

Scatter the almonds over the base of a baking dish and toast for 7–8 minutes in an oven preheated to 180°C fan/200°C/gas mark 6.

Just before serving, arrange a few amaretti in the centre, scatter most of the flaked almonds over, with a few around the edge, and dust with icing sugar.

This trifle's a voyage of jelly and custard, with strains of spicy mulled wine, or muddled wine as my son would have it, and little jellied fruit slices that complete the punchbowl effect.

mulled wine trifle

Base

150ml sweet white wine

50ml brandy

100ml fresh smooth orange juice

6 cloves

2 star anise

1 cinnamon stick

50g white caster sugar

2 gelatine leaves, e.g. Supercook,
   cut into broad strips (or ½ an 11g
   sachet of powdered gelatine,
   see page 147)

approx. 6 trifle sponges

150g raspberry jam

Custard

4 medium egg yolks

80g icing sugar, sifted

50g plain flour, sifted

425ml full-cream milk

2 strips of orange peel, removed
   with a potato peeler

On Top

300ml double cream

jellied orange and lemon slices

Serves 8

Bring the wine, brandy, orange juice, spices and sugar to the boil in a small saucepan. Stir to dissolve the sugar, then leave to infuse for 5 minutes. In the meantime, place the gelatine in a bowl, cover with cold water and leave to soak for 5 minutes, then drain. Pour some of the hot wine solution over the soaked gelatine, stir until it dissolves, then stir this back into the rest of the solution.

Arrange the trifle sponges over the base of a 20cm trifle bowl 8–9cm deep, cutting them to fit. Strain over the wine solution, leave to cool, then cover and chill for several hours or until set.

In the meantime make the custard. Whisk the egg yolks and icing sugar together in a medium-size non-stick saucepan until smooth, then whisk in the flour a third at a time, until you have a thick creamy paste. Bring the milk to the boil in a small saucepan with the orange peel, and whisk it into the egg mixture a little at a time to begin with, until it is all incorporated. Return the pan to a low heat and cook for a few minutes until the custard thickens, stirring vigorously with a wooden spoon to disperse any lumps that form; if necessary you can give it a quick whisk. The custard shouldn't actually boil, but the odd bubble will ensure that it's hot enough to thicken properly. Cook it for a few minutes longer, again stirring constantly. Discard the orange zest, pour the custard into a bowl, cover the surface with clingfilm and leave to cool.

To assemble the trifle, work the jam in a bowl to loosen it, then spread it over the surface of the sponges and jelly. Give the custard a stir with a spoon to smooth it, and spread this over the jam. Whisk the cream in a bowl until it forms soft peaks and spread it over the top of the custard. Cover and chill for a couple of hours or overnight. Decorate with jellied slices just before serving.

Panettone could have been created especially for bread and butter pud – replete with dried fruit and candied peel, it turns an old favourite into a Christmas great. A nice plump loaf should still leave plenty for teatime.

pear and panettone pudding

3 medium eggs
150g golden caster sugar
425ml double cream
425ml full-cream milk
1 tablespoon dark rum (optional)
salted butter, softened
10–12 x 1cm slices of panettone (cut as wedges from a 500–750g loaf)
2 slightly underripe pears, peeled, quartered, cored and sliced lengthways
90g apricot jam, warmed and sieved (optional)

Serves 6

Preheat the oven to 160°C fan/180°C/gas mark 4. Whisk the eggs and sugar in a bowl, then whisk in the cream, milk and rum. Butter the panettone and arrange lengthways in overlapping slices to cover the base of a 35cm/2.6 litre oval gratin or other shallow ovenproof dish. The centre may take two slices side by side, while the narrow ends will only hold one. Scatter the pears over the top. Pour the custard through a sieve over and around the panettone and fruit.

Place the gratin dish in a roasting dish with cold water that comes two-thirds of the way up the sides. Bake for 1 hour, until the custard is puffy and set and the bread golden. Brush the surface of the bread with the apricot jam (this bit is optional but it gives the pudding a lovely sticky glaze). Serve straight away.

This is one of those rich and glam chocolate creations that will either make a louche tea-time treat or a soignée pud. I can never resist the shimmer of gold and silver dragées, Smarties and the like, and this is just the right place to show them off.

tira-mi-su torte

Cake

50g self-raising flour
50g light muscovado sugar
50ml groundnut oil
1 medium egg, separated
1 tablespoon espresso, or very strong
   black coffee, cooled
1 tablespoon full cream milk

Filling

300g dark chocolate (approx. 50%
   cocoa), broken into pieces
4 medium organic eggs, separated
30g golden caster sugar
250g mascarpone
2 tablespoons Kahlua or very
   strong black coffee
edible gold or silver decorations,
   e.g. Smarties, dragées, chocolate
   stars or leaf

Serves 6–8

Preheat the oven to 170°C fan/190°C/gas mark 5 and butter a 20cm cake tin at least 4cm deep with a removable base. Sift the flour and sugar into a medium-size bowl. Add the oil, egg yolk, espresso and milk and beat with a wooden spoon until smooth. Whisk the egg white until stiff in another bowl, I use a hand-held electric whisk for this, and fold into the mixture in two goes. Spoon this into the prepared tin, covering the base evenly, and give the tin a couple of sharp taps on the work surface to allow any bubbles to rise. Bake in the oven for 12–15 minutes until lightly golden, firm when pressed and shrinking from the sides. Leave to cool.

Place the chocolate in a bowl set over a pan with a little simmering water in it and gently melt. Remove the bowl from the heat and leave the chocolate to cool to room temperature if necessary. Whisk the egg whites until stiff in a largish bowl, then whisk the egg yolks and sugar in another bowl until very pale and mousse-like.

Add the mascarpone to the melted chocolate and blend, then fold in the egg yolk mixture, and then the egg whites in two goes. Stir in the Kahlua or coffee. Smooth the chocolate cream over the cake base, cover and chill for several hours or overnight. Decorate with gold or silver decorations, run a knife around the collar and remove it, and serve the torte in slices.

An unctuously creamy white chocolate cheesecake that panders to our aspirations for a white Christmas. This is very much a pud, and would be delicious served with a little fruit compote, a cranberry one for dramatics.

white christmas cheesecake

Crust

50g unsalted butter

150g plain digestives

Filling

4 gelatine leaves, e.g. Supercook, cut into broad strips (or 1 x 11g sachet of powdered gelatine, see page 147)

400g crème fraîche

100g white caster sugar

1 teaspoon vanilla extract

75g white chocolate, e.g. Green & Black's, broken into pieces

400g ricotta

white chocolate shavings to decorate

Serves 6–8
Makes 1 x 20cm cake

Gently melt the butter in a small saucepan over a low heat. Place the digestives inside a plastic bag and crush them to fine crumbs using a rolling pin. Tip them into the saucepan with the melted butter and stir to coat them, then transfer to a 20cm cake tin 9cm deep with a removable base. Using your fingers or the bottom of a tumbler, press them into the base, making sure you seal the edges, and place in the fridge while you do the next stage.

Place the gelatine in a bowl, cover with cold water and soak for 5 minutes, then drain. Pour 3 tablespoons of boiling water over the soaked gelatine and stir to dissolve. Place the crème fraîche in a small saucepan with the sugar and gently heat, stirring constantly with a wooden spoon until the mixture liquefies and the sugar has dissolved. Give the mixture a quick whisk to get rid of any lumps. It should be warm, roughly the same temperature as the gelatine solution. Stir the gelatine into the crème fraîche mixture, along with the vanilla extract, then transfer to a bowl and leave to cool.

Gently melt the chocolate in a bowl set over a pan with a little simmering water in it. Place the ricotta in the bowl of a food processor and whiz until smooth, add the melted chocolate and whiz again, then add the cream and sugar mixture and whiz once more. Pour this mixture on top of the cheesecake base. Cover with clingfilm and chill overnight. Decorate with chocolate shavings before serving.

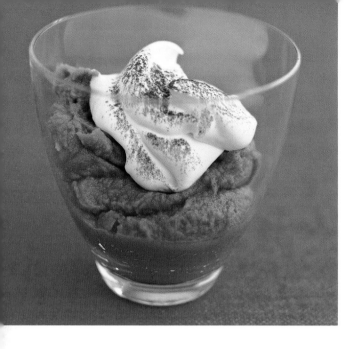

An instant, luxurious and hedonistic affair in the company of whipped cream (or Chantilly, to give it a lacy name), and meringues – most good pâtisseries sell big cloud-like over-sized ones that make for glamorous rustic eating.

mont blanc in a glass

1 x 435g tin of unsweetened
    chestnut purée
4 tablespoons golden syrup
2 tablespoons dark rum
200ml double cream
cocoa for dusting
meringues to serve

Serves 6

Whiz the chestnut purée, syrup and rum in a food processor until smooth. Divide between six 125ml glasses, mounding it with a tablespoon. Whisk the cream to firm peaks in a bowl, I use a hand-held electric whisk, and dollop a heaped tablespoon in a mound on top of the chestnut purée. Dust with cocoa, cover and chill until required. The pud can be made a day in advance. Serve with the meringues.

Effortlessly chic, traditionally vanilla ice cream with hot chocolate sauce and meringue, here the 'dame' in question is wearing her mantle on the reverse side in the Christmas spirit of things, in other words a dark chocolate ice cream with a white chocolate sauce.

dame blanche

½ x 500ml tub of chocolate
   ice cream
4 meringue nests
100ml whipping cream, whisked
   to fluffy peaks
cocoa for dusting

Sauce

75g white chocolate, e.g. Green
   & Black's, broken into pieces
75ml single cream
1 tablespoon Cointreau or
   Grand Marnier

Serves 4

To make the chocolate sauce, gently melt the chocolate, cream and liqueur in a bowl set over a pan with a little simmering water in it, stirring until smooth.

Remove the ice cream from the freezer 10–15 minutes before serving to allow it to soften. Place the meringue nests on four plates, with a scoop of chocolate ice cream in the centre of each one, and a fluffy mound of cream on top. Dust with cocoa and serve the hot chocolate sauce separately in a little jug or bowl.

A rich cranberry and orange ice cream that can be made without any churning, with chocolate sauce for diehards. In fact the sauce is good for any ice cream you happen to have in the freezer, should your offspring insist it comes in a tub. Both the sauces are optional with the parfait, which is lovely on its own too.

cranberry and orange parfait

200g golden caster sugar

zest of 2 oranges, removed with
   a potato peeler

250ml fresh orange juice

150g cranberries

450ml double cream

9 medium organic egg yolks

**Serves 8
Makes 1 x 22cm parfait**

Place the sugar and orange zest in a small saucepan with the orange juice and cranberries. Bring to the boil over a medium-high heat and cook for 35–45 minutes, until you have a thick syrup (it should register 115°C or 'soft ball' on a jam thermometer). Towards the end of this time, whisk the cream in a large bowl until stiff.

Tip the contents of the pan into a sieve set over a bowl, pressing down on the cranberries. Put the egg yolks into a food processor and drizzle in the syrup with the motor running. Continue to whisk for a couple of minutes until the mixture turns pale and creamy, then transfer it to a large mixing bowl and stir for a minute or so until it cools to blood or room temperature.

Whisk the cream into the egg yolk mixture in two goes, then transfer it to a 22cm/1.3 litre loaf tin, cover and freeze overnight. Remove from the freezer about 20 minutes before eating. To turn out, briefly dip the base of the terrine into a sink of hot water, run a knife around the sides and invert. Serve in slices with the chocolate sauce and a teaspoon of the cranberry purée.

chocolate sauce

150g dark chocolate (approx. 70%
   cocoa), broken into pieces

150ml full cream milk

50ml single cream

2 tablespoons Cointreau

30g icing sugar, sifted

Gently melt the chocolate in a bowl set over a pan with a little simmering water in it, then whisk in the milk in two goes, and then the cream, Cointreau and icing sugar. Pour into a clean bowl, cover and chill for several hours. Stir well before serving.

cranberry purée

200g cranberry sauce

1 tablespoon lemon juice

Gently warm the cranberry sauce in a small saucepan until it loosens, then press it through a sieve into a bowl. Stir in the lemon juice, cover and leave to cool.

This jelly is for when you have all but given up on getting anything even vaguely healthy down your sugar-saturated offspring, although you're permitted a small shot glass of iced eau-de-vie poured over yours. It's a cheering Christmas-red, and plays the part turned out of a vintage jelly mould.

cranberry jelly

150g cranberries

4 tablespoons fresh orange juice

75g white caster sugar

6 gelatine leaves, e.g. Supercook,
  cut into broad strips (or 1½ x 11g
  sachets of powdered gelatine*)

approx. 600ml cranberry juice

Serves 4–6

Place the cranberries in a small saucepan with the orange juice and sugar. Bring to the boil, then cover and cook over a low heat for 8–10 minutes, until the berries have softened. At the same time, place the gelatine strips in a medium-size bowl, cover with cold water and leave to soak for 5 minutes, then drain.

Press the contents of the pan through a sieve on top of the gelatine, and stir until it dissolves. Gradually stir in the cranberry juice, and make up to 750ml with a little more juice if necessary. Rinse a 750ml mould or bowl with water (you can also use individual moulds or ramekins should you prefer). Pour in the jelly solution and chill overnight until set.

To unmould the jelly, briefly dip the mould into a sink of hot water, place a plate on top and invert it.

*If using powdered gelatine, sprinkle it on to about 3 tablespoons of boiling water in a small bowl, leave for 3–4 minutes and then stir to dissolve. If the gelatine has not completely dissolved, stand the bowl in another bowl of just-boiled water for a few minutes, then stir again. Alternatively set the bowl over a pan with a little simmering water in it.

baking

Of all the Christmas cooking to be done, it's the baking that I most enjoy – it brings the memories of those childhood Christmases flooding back. Dark afternoons spent in a warm kitchen rolling out pastry for mince pies, with the heady scent of brandy or rum, cinnamon, cloves, allspice and ginger, and the Christmas tree shimmering in the distance, are just pure magic. And when there are children in the house, you can cut the excitement with a knife, as the countdown to their agonisingly long wait nears its end.

Mince pies are a must. But I've gone full circle on these and decided that actually I do quite like the unreconstructed type, pastry rolled that little bit too thick AND with a lid. Providing that is, it's very good pastry, short, crumbly and sweet, and not unlike a biscuit. Using half lard and half butter may make the health-conscious shudder (and there's no reason why it shouldn't be all butter), but the combination does make for meltingly flaky pastry. A plate of these also makes a great present. I try to pencil a mince pie afternoon into my diary, so that I can bake up a few dozen.

A traditional Christmas cake can feel like doubling up on the mince pies, although in our house we seem to have a bottomless appetite for both. A sliver of fruit cake with farmhouse Cheddar is essential Christmas grazing. This cake is something in the way of wonder: there are no eggs, and there's no added sugar. For others, though, a very gooey festive chocolate cake may appeal more, which will double up as a pud. And it's hard to resist a little in the way of fantasy baking – children will love this Santa's grotto cake with its marshmallow frosting and sweeties. Actually it tastes quite good too. And while you're making the mince pies, it's only one step on to a batch of spicy biscuits to hang on the tree.

Enough of new 'takes' on mince pies. There is something that strokes the soul in a good old-fashioned one, the kind that's passed round the church hall after a carol service, with a proper lid dusted with caster sugar and that little bit too much pastry. The lard is a British touch that allows for really short pastry, and there's no need to make your own mincemeat unless you want to. These can be stored in an airtight container for up to a week, and can also be frozen.

good old-fashioned mince pies

1–2 tablespoons brandy
a squeeze of lemon juice
approx. 300g best-quality mincemeat
golden caster sugar for dusting

Pastry
450g plain flour
125g unsalted butter, chilled
   and diced
125g lard, chilled and diced
100g icing sugar, sifted
1 medium egg yolk
milk or water, to brush the top

Makes approx. 18

To make the pastry, place the flour, butter and lard in a food processor, give it a quick burst at high speed to reduce it to a crumb-like consistency, then add the icing sugar and give it another quick burst. Add the egg yolk and enough milk or water to bring the dough together, wrap it in clingfilm and chill for 1 hour or overnight.

Preheat the oven to 170°C fan/190°C/gas mark 5. Stir the brandy and lemon juice into the mincemeat. Roll two-thirds of the pastry the thickness of a pound coin, 3–4mm, on a lightly floured work surface, and cut out circles using an 8cm fluted cutter to fit a couple of fairy cake trays (ideally non-stick). Place these in the tins and fill with a heaped teaspoon of mincemeat.

Roll out the remaining pastry with the trimmings and cut out lids using a 6cm fluted cutter. Brush the rim of the pies with milk or water, lay the lids on top and gently press the edges together. Dust with sugar and bake for 15–20 minutes, until the pastry is a pale gold. Serve warm, about 20 minutes out of the oven, or at room temperature. They can also be reheated for 5 minutes in an oven preheated to 150°C fan/170°C/gas mark 3. A little brandy butter (see page 128) on top or slipped under the lid while they're warm keeps them in traditional mode, with or without the rum sauce for pud.

Unless you are planning on taking a two-week break before the big day, the chances are you won't have time to make a gingerbread house. But we can have mini iced ginger buns with little in the way of fuss, it's the essential spice that we're after.

mini gingerbread buns

4 tablespoons lager

90g dark muscovado sugar

1/8 teaspoon bicarbonate of soda

70g self-raising flour

1 level teaspoon ground ginger

1 medium egg

3 tablespoons groundnut
  or vegetable oil

fine white writing icing

Makes approx. 15

Preheat the oven to 160°C fan/180°C/gas mark 4, and arrange about fifteen paper mini muffin cases in one or two mini muffin trays. Alternatively arrange double cases, one inside the other, on a baking sheet. Bring the lager and muscovado sugar to the boil in a small saucepan, working out any lumps with the back of a spoon. Remove from the heat and stir in the bicarbonate of soda, then set aside while you prepare the cake batter.

Sift the flour and ginger into a bowl. Whisk together the egg and oil in another bowl, then slowly add this to the flour, stirring. Add the beer mixture in two goes, gently mixing it in. Three-quarters fill each muffin case and bake for approx. 15 minutes, until risen, firm and starting to colour. Remove and leave them to cool, then decorate with a zigzag of spidery white icing and little icing dots. These cakes will keep well in an airtight container for several days.

These individual fruit cakes with a buttery crumble on top will appeal to those who find Christmas cake that little bit too dark and full of dried fruits. These are delicious eaten slightly warm, with a dollop of rum or brandy butter (see page 128).

christmas crumble muffins

Crumble

70g light muscovado sugar
70g unsalted butter, chilled and diced
100g plain flour
1/3 teaspoon ground cinnamon

Cake

180g unsalted butter, diced
180g light muscovado sugar
3 medium eggs, plus 1 yolk
50ml dark rum
80g currants
40g diced candied peel
40g undyed glacé cherries, sliced
180g plain flour
¾ teaspoon baking powder
icing sugar for dusting

Makes 12

Preheat the oven to 170°C fan/190°C/gas mark 5, and arrange twelve paper muffin cases in a muffin tray. Place all the ingredients for the crumble in the bowl of a food processor and whiz to fine crumbs, then transfer the mixture to a bowl.

To make the cake mixture, place the butter and sugar in the bowl of a food processor and cream for several minutes until fluffy. Add the eggs and the yolk one at a time, scraping down the bowl if necessary, then incorporate the rum (don't worry if the mixture appears curdled at this point). Transfer to a large bowl. Toss the currants, peel and cherries with a little flour to coat them. Sift the remaining flour and baking powder over the cake mixture and gently fold in, followed by the dried and candied fruits.

Spoon the cake mixture into the paper cases, half filling them, and scatter the crumble over the top. Bake the cakes for 25 minutes, until risen and lightly golden on the surface. Leave to cool, then dust with icing sugar. These are at their yummiest the day they are made, when the crumble is crisp, but they can also be stored for a day or two. A plastic food bag, loosely tied, is preferable to an airtight container.

Dense, fudgy chocolate cakes are ever the hallmark of luxury, and this won't let you down, with its hint of hazelnuts and rum or coffee in what is otherwise full-on chocolate.

chocolate fudge drizzle cake

Cake

200g unsalted butter, diced

200g dark chocolate (approx. 50% cocoa), broken into pieces

3 tablespoons dark rum, espresso or strong black coffee

4 medium eggs, separated

125g light muscovado sugar

40g ground almonds

½ teaspoon sea salt

40g skinned hazelnuts

icing sugar for dusting

Icing

25g dark muscovado sugar

1 tablespoon double cream

25g dark chocolate, broken into pieces

25g unsalted butter

Makes 1 x 20cm cake

Preheat the oven to 160°C fan/180°C/gas mark 4, and butter a 20cm cake tin 9cm deep with a removable base. Melt the butter, chocolate and rum or coffee in a bowl set over a pan of simmering water, stirring occasionally. Whisk the egg whites in a bowl until stiff, then gradually whisk in half the sugar, a tablespoon at a time, whisking for about 20 seconds with each addition, until by the end you have a stiff, glossy meringue. Whisk the egg yolks with the remaining sugar in a large bowl for several minutes until pale and doubled in volume. Transfer the mixture to a bowl.

Fold the chocolate and butter into the egg and sugar mixture, lightly fold in the ground almonds with the salt, then fold in the egg whites in two goes. Pour the mixture into the prepared tin, give it a couple of taps on the work surface to bring up any large air bubbles, and bake for 40–45 minutes until a skewer inserted into the centre comes out clean. Run a knife around the edge of the cake and leave it to cool in the tin. Meanwhile, spread the nuts over the base of a small baking dish and toast for about 15 minutes until golden. Leave to cool and then coarsely chop.

Invert the cake on to a plate and remove the base (you will be icing the bottom rather than the top). To make the icing, heat the muscovado sugar and cream together for several minutes in a bowl set over a pan of simmering water, until completely smooth. Add the chocolate and butter and continue to heat, whisking until glossy and blended. Trickle the icing over the cake, so that it runs down the sides as well, and scatter with the nuts. Leave to set for a couple of hours. It will keep well in a covered container for several days. You may like to give it a light dusting of icing sugar before serving.

all gold christmas cake

Homemade marzipan is as delicate and pretty as commercial marzipan is overpowering and garish. The real thing has a restrained scent of almonds, the gentlest hint of brandy and lemon, and is a pale ivory in colour. In fact there's no need for icing at all, I'd stop right there. But I would invest in a small pot of edible gold powder, which is available from cake specialists (see page 9). It lasts for years, so you can put it away with the tree decorations and get it out again next year.

This is a lovely moist and sticky fruit cake that draws all its sweetness from dates and dried fruits. It will appeal to those who like really dark fruit cakes. Feed it with teasing teaspoons of Calvados or brandy in the run-up to Christmas, so it becomes richer and deeper by the week. Peeling back the layers of crinkly baking paper and drawing in its heady scent is a treat of a ritual. That said, it can also be eaten straight away, but otherwise, if you're heeding tradition on 'Stir-up Sunday' and making a pud, why not make the cake at the same time?

300g unsalted butter
500ml apple juice
300g pitted and chopped dates
350g raisins
325g sultanas
1 teaspoon bicarbonate of soda
150g plain flour, sifted
150g ground almonds
½ teaspoon freshly grated nutmeg
½ teaspoon ground cinnamon
finely grated zest of 1 orange
   and 1 lemon
approx. 2 tablespoons Calvados or brandy,
   for feeding the cake

Marzipan
200g ground almonds
200g icing sugar
1 teaspoon lemon juice
1 teaspoon Calvados or brandy
1 medium organic egg white

Decoration
100g apricot jam
edible gold powder, a thick gold ribbon,
   strings of gold beads (optional)

Makes 1 x 20cm cake

Melt the butter in a medium-size saucepan with the apple juice, then stir in the dates, raisins and sultanas, bring to the boil and simmer over a low heat for 5 minutes. Transfer the mixture to a large mixing bowl and stir in the bicarbonate of soda (the mixture will sizzle furiously), then leave it to cool for 10 minutes.

Preheat the oven to 140°C fan/160°C/gas mark 2½, and butter a 20cm cake tin 9cm deep, with a removable base. Line the bottom with baking paper, and butter this also. Beat the flour, ground almonds, nutmeg and cinnamon into the dried fruit mixture. Fold in the zest and transfer the mixture to the cake tin, smoothing the surface.

Tear off a sheet of baking paper large enough to cover the surface of the cake and go about halfway down the sides of the tin. Cut out a small circle from the centre about 2cm in diameter, then butter the surface that will come in contact with the cake as it rises. Lay it over the top of the tin and tie it in place with string. Bake the cake for 2½ hours, until a skewer inserted into the centre comes out clean – it will be a very deep brown at this point. Leave the cake to cool, then run a knife around the collar, remove it from the base and peel off the bottom paper.

The cake will be good to eat from the following day onwards. If maturing it, however, pierce the top all over with a skewer and feed it with a teaspoon of Calvados or brandy, then wrap it in a double layer of first baking paper and then foil. Continue to feed it at weekly intervals for about 6 weeks. You can step the booze up to a couple of teaspoons at a time if maturing it for a few weeks only.

To make the marzipan, place all the ingredients except the egg white in the bowl of a food processor and whiz together, then add the egg white and bring together into a pliable paste. Wrap the marzipan in clingfilm and chill until required. Hang on to the bowl that contained the egg white, as you need just a little for the decoration.

Gently heat the jam in a small saucepan, press it through a sieve and very lightly glaze the cake using a pastry brush – again hang on to the bowl. Measure the cake from the base of one side to the base of the other. Thinly roll out the marzipan on a work surface dusted with icing sugar into a circle a little bigger than this, about 30cm in diameter. Loosen it with a palette knife every now and again, and dust the surface with icing sugar as necessary, but avoid dusting the top. Roll the marzipan around the rolling pin, lift it up and carefully lay it on top of the cake, letting it drape down the sides. Press it to the sides of the cake, cut out darts where folds appear and smooth these with your fingers, then trim it at base level.

Roll out the trimmings and cut out about three holly leaves using a biscuit cutter or template, and make little balls as berries. Dab a little jam on to the base of these using the residual jam in the bowl and arrange on top of the cake. Brush the tops of the balls and the edge of the leaves with a little of the egg white left in the bowl, using a small brush, and dust with gold powder, again using a fine brush. Tie a big gold ribbon around the outside, and some strings of gold beads should you have any. Set the cake aside and leave overnight for the marzipan to semi-dry, then store in an airtight container.

This cake is my way of sneaking a poinsettia into the house, as they don't really feature on my landscape architect husband's radar. But he probably wouldn't mind eating it, a moist hazelnut sponge with a moussey cinnamon butter icing.

You can turn it down still further by making the flowers with white icing. But for the full on effect it's either ready-to-roll red icing, or you can make the flowers by kneading about a teaspoon of red food colouring liquid into 200g marzipan to dye it pink. Thinly roll this out on a work surface lightly dusted with icing sugar, cut out poinsettia leaves and decorate the cake. Using fine red writing icing, trace in the outside of the leaves and the veins.

poinsettia cake

Sponge
350g roasted chopped hazelnuts*
6 medium eggs, separated
250g golden caster sugar
1½ teaspoons baking powder

Filling
100g unsalted butter, softened
50g icing sugar
½ teaspoon ground cinnamon
100g thick ready-prepared custard

Icing and Decoration
580g ready-to-roll white icing
100g apricot jam
gold, red, green or white ribbon
   and gold balls to decorate

Makes 1 x 20cm cake

To prepare the sponge, preheat the oven to 180°C fan/200°C/gas mark 6, and butter two 20cm cake tins at least 4cm deep with a removable base. Grind the nuts in batches in a coffee grinder, taking care to stop the motor before they turn to a paste at the bottom. Whisk the egg yolks and sugar together in a large bowl – the mixture should not be too pale and thick. Stiffly whisk the egg whites and gently fold them into the mixture in three goes. Fold in the ground nuts and the baking powder.

Divide the cake mixture between the tins and give them a couple of taps on the work surface to bring up any air bubbles. Bake for approximately 25 minutes, until the top feels springy to the touch and the cake is shrinking away from the sides. A skewer inserted into the centre should come out clean. Remove the collar from the cakes and leave to cool.

Using an electric whisk, beat the softened butter in a medium-size bowl until creamy and almost white. If it's on the hard side you can cream it in a food processor first. Sift over the sugar and cinnamon and fold in, then gradually whisk in the custard and continue whisking for another few minutes, on a low speed to begin with and then on a higher speed, until it is fluffy and mousse-like.

If the sides of the cakes are particularly high, trim the edges with a bread knife. Remove the sponges from their base and invert them, then spread the top of one with the buttercream and sandwich with the second one. Measure the cake from the base of one side to the base of the other. Thinly roll out 450g of the icing on a work surface dusted with icing sugar into a circle a little bigger than this, about 35cm in diameter. Loosen it with a palette knife every now and again, and dust the surface with icing sugar as necessary, but avoid dusting the top.

Gently heat the jam in a small saucepan until it liquefies, press it through a sieve and use it to brush the top and sides of the cake. Roll the icing around the rolling pin, lift it up and carefully drape over the cake, pressing it to the sides. Cut out darts from the side where there is excess icing and smooth the edges together, then trim the base.

Cut out a poinsettia leaf about 7cm in length from a piece of paper (if in doubt about their shape, then google an image, or refer to a Christmas card). Roll out the remaining icing as thinly as possible in the same way as before, and cut out some leaves. Use these to decorate the top of the cake, securing them with a little jam. Tie a thick ribbon around the outside. The cake will keep well for several days in a cool place, loosely covered with clingfilm, or in an airtight container.

*You can also use ground almonds, or ground toasted almonds. Arrange flaked almonds in a thin layer on baking sheets and toast for 9–10 minutes at 180°C fan/200°C/gas mark 6, then cool. These, however, tend to be a little oilier when you grind them.

'It's a marshmallow world in the winter', or so we wish. This is one to have fun with – decorate it with marshmallow snowmen, chocolate coins and candy sticks and it will be every child's idea of a dream Christmas cake. But otherwise raid the sweetie counter for jelly beans, flumps, marshmallow twists and jelly loops. White marshmallows will give a suitably snowy frosting, and pink ones a pale Barbie-doll blush.

santa's grotto cake

Cake

225g unsalted butter, diced
225g golden caster sugar
225g self-raising flour
2 teaspoons baking powder
finely grated zest of 1 orange
4 medium eggs
100ml fresh smooth orange juice

Frosting

2 medium organic egg whites
150g white caster sugar
2 tablespoons fresh smooth
   orange juice
½ teaspoon cream of tartar
pinch of sea salt
11 pink or white marshmallows, halved
selection of marshmallows, chocolate
   coins and candy sticks to decorate

Makes 1 x 20cm cake

Preheat the oven to 170°C fan/190°C/gas mark 5, and butter a 20cm cake tin 9cm deep with a removable base. Place all the cake ingredients in the bowl of a food processor and cream together. Transfer the mixture to the cake tin, smoothing the surface, and bake for 50–55 minutes, or until a skewer inserted into the centre comes out clean. Run a knife around the collar of the cake and leave it to cool. You can leave the cake on the base or remove it as you prefer.

To make the frosting, blend the egg whites, sugar, orange juice, cream of tartar and salt in a large bowl, using an electric whisk. Set the bowl over a pan with a little simmering water in it and whisk at high speed for 5 minutes, until you have a thick, mousse-like glaze that stands in peaks. Add the marshmallows and stir for several minutes until they begin to soften and melt, then whisk until the mixture is smooth and they have completely melted, and remove from the heat.

Spread the frosting thickly over the top and sides of the cake using a palette knife, though you may not need quite all of it. Decorate with the sweeties and set aside for a couple of hours. The cake will keep well for several days in an airtight container.

A bûche de Noël is the French equivalent of our Christmas pudding, and in typical style has glamorous all-round potential, like so much of their pâtisserie.

bûche de noël

Sponge
50g cocoa
a pinch of sea salt
3 large eggs
75g light muscovado sugar

Filling
75g dark chocolate (approx. 70% cocoa), broken into pieces
375g unsweetened chestnut purée
60g light muscovado sugar
1½ teaspoons vanilla extract
180ml whipping cream

Christmas figurines to decorate
icing sugar for dusting

Serves 6–8

To make the sponge, preheat the oven to 180°C fan/200°C/gas mark 6. Butter a 23 x 32cm Swiss roll tin, line it with baking paper and butter this also. Sift the cocoa into a bowl and add the salt. Place the eggs and muscovado sugar in a bowl and whisk for 8–10 minutes, using an electric whisk, until the mixture is pale and mousse-like. Lightly fold in the cocoa in two goes. Pour the mixture into the prepared tin and smooth it using a palette knife. Give the tin a couple of sharp taps on the work surface to eliminate any large air bubbles and bake the sponge for 8–10 minutes, until set and springy to the touch.

Lay out a clean tea towel and sift over a fine layer of icing sugar. Turn the cake out on to it and carefully roll it up with the tea towel, leaving the paper in place, starting at the short end so you end up with a short fat roll. Leave to cool for 40–60 minutes.

To make the filling, gently melt the chocolate in a bowl set over a pan of simmering water, then set it aside to cool to room temperature. Cream the chestnut purée, sugar and vanilla in a food processor, then add the chocolate. Whip the cream until it forms soft peaks, and fold it into the chocolate chestnut mixture in two goes.

Carefully unroll the sponge and peel off the paper parchment. Spread with half the chocolate chestnut mousse, then roll the sponge up again and tip it on to a long serving plate, seam downwards. You could also line a small board with silver foil and decorate the edge. Smooth the rest of the filling over, then make lines along its length with a fork, swirling the ends to create a log effect, and making a few knots on the log too. Decorate it with your favourite Christmas figurines.

Chill the roulade for an hour; if keeping it for longer than this, loosely cover it with clingfilm and bring it back up to room temperature for 30 minutes before eating. Shortly before serving, shower the log with icing sugar.

A guiding light for Santa as well as the Magi, we leave these out with the essential nip of something fiery or a glass of milk and a pile of moss for the reindeers on Christmas Eve.

star of bethlehem biscuits

140g plain flour
60g golden caster sugar
120g unsalted butter, diced
1/4 teaspoon vanilla extract
1 medium egg yolk, beaten
10g cocoa, sifted
groundnut or vegetable oil for brushing
20g dark chocolate (approx. 70% cocoa), broken into pieces
icing sugar for dusting (optional)

Makes approx. 15

Place 80g of the flour, half the sugar and half the butter in the bowl of a food processor and briefly whiz until the mixture is crumblike. Add the vanilla and half the egg yolk and whiz again until the mixture comes together into a ball. Wrap in clingfilm and chill for at least an hour. Make a second batch of dough with the remaining flour, sugar, butter and egg yolk in the same way, adding the cocoa to the food processor with the flour (and omitting any vanilla). Chill this too.

Preheat the oven to 170°C fan/190°C/gas mark 5, and brush a couple of baking trays with oil. Thinly roll out each dough in turn on a lightly floured work surface, rotating it as necessary, very lightly sprinkling the top with a little flour to stop the rolling pin sticking. Cut out stars using a 6cm cutter and arrange on baking trays, rolling the dough twice. Bake for approx. 10 minutes, until lightly coloured, then remove and immediately loosen with a metal spatula – if you leave them even a few minutes they will break as you remove them. Leave to cool.

Gently melt the chocolate in a small saucepan over a low heat. Using a pastry brush, dab a little in the centre of each vanilla biscuit, then sandwich with a chocolate one so the points of the stars are alternated. If you like, lightly dust the tops with icing sugar, using a tea-strainer. Set aside in a cool place for about an hour for the chocolate to harden. These will keep well in an airtight container for several days.

Hanging the tree with spiced biscuits is one of those Martha Stewart moments that we are inclined to experience at this time of year, however lapsed we may be during the rest of it. The good bit being that you can get your children to make them: older ones can do the baking while younger ones can decorate them. But it's worth saving the hanging until Christmas Eve or just before, not only to keep them fresh, as they soften within a day, but because otherwise, as with tree chocolates, the tree will have been denuded come Christmas Day.

You will need a set of cutters, anything from holly leaves, bells, snowflakes, snowmen, stockings and stars (see page 9 for stockists). Also some thin ribbon for hanging them.

christmas tree biscuits

50g unsalted butter
100g golden caster sugar
100g runny honey
225g plain flour
½ teaspoon baking powder
½ teaspoon bicarbonate of soda
1 teaspoon each ground ginger
   and cinnamon
½ beaten medium egg
vegetable oil for brushing
white writing icing to decorate
silver balls (optional)

Makes 20–30

Gently heat the butter, sugar and honey together in a small saucepan, stirring until melted and smooth. Working off the heat, add the dry ingredients and stir until crumbly, then add the egg and work to a dough. If it seems very sticky you can add a little more flour. Tip this on to a work surface, bring it into a ball, then pat it between your palms until you have a pleasingly smooth and shiny dough. Wrap it in clingfilm, leave to cool, then chill for several hours or overnight.

Preheat the oven to 160°C fan/180°C/gas mark 4, and brush a couple of baking sheets with vegetable oil. Thinly roll out the dough on a lightly floured work surface to a thickness of about 2mm and cut out the desired shapes using biscuit cutters. Roll the dough twice, arranging the biscuits on the baking trays – they don't spread much, so you can place them quite close together. If you are planning on hanging them, make a hole at the top of each one using a skewer.

Bake the biscuits for 10–12 minutes until an even pale gold; the lower tray may take longer than the upper one. The holes will have closed up a little, so make them a bit larger using the skewer. Now loosen the biscuits with a palette knife – it's important to do this straight away, before they harden and become brittle. Transfer to a rack to cool. Ice and decorate them as you fancy, and leave to set for an hour or two. They can be stored in an airtight container, un-iced or iced, for several weeks. Thread them with thin ribbon if you are planning on hanging them.

Just when you thought it was all over, another cake, traditionally served in France on Epiphany to celebrate the arrival of the Magi in Bethlehem to honour the baby Jesus. It is also known as Twelfth Night cake. Just as we hide a coin in our Christmas pudding, a small figurine known as 'la fève' is inserted into the filling (most likely plastic these days), and whoever finds it in their slice is crowned king for a day, which when there are children present means some discreet digging around on the part of whoever is serving it to make sure it goes to the right person. I usually dish this up for New Year's Eve dinner, when the kings are still journeying, as the cake is served in the few days up to and beyond Epiphany. And with it a spoonful of crème fraîche, brandy butter or the rum sauce on page 128.

galette des rois

125g unsalted butter, softened
125g golden caster sugar
100g ground almonds
50g plain flour
finely grated zest of 1 lemon
2 medium eggs
1 tablespoon dark rum (optional)
1 tablespoon milk
approx. 375g puff pastry

Serves 6–8

Preheat the oven to 200°C fan/220°C/gas mark 7. To make the filling, blend the butter, sugar and ground almonds in a food processor, then add the flour, lemon zest, one of the eggs and an egg white, and the rum if including. You should have a creamy spreadable paste. Blend the remaining egg yolk with the milk.

Thinly roll out half the pastry on a lightly floured work surface to a thickness of about 2mm, and cut out a 25cm circle using a plate as a guide. Spread the filling to within 3cm of the edge. If you like you can push a little figure or a coin into the mixture. Roll out the second half of the pastry a couple of centimetres larger all round than the first circle. Paint the lower rim with egg wash, lay the second pastry circle on top and press the edges together, then trim the top circle level with the lower one. Paint the pie all over with the egg wash and fold in the rim, then paint this too. Mark the surface with the prongs of a fork in diagonal lines, and the rim, and cut a slit in the surface to allow the steam to escape.

Bake the pie for 20 minutes until golden and risen. Serve warm about 15 minutes out of the oven. It can also be reheated for about 20 minutes at 150°C fan/170°C/gas mark 3.

chocs
and gifts

Beautiful chocolates are central to the celebrations. In fact one of the first signs that Christmas is upon us is the windows of French pâtisseries, dressed to the nines, which hold the food-obsessed among us in awe in the run-up with every espresso stopover. It's not so much the twinkling display of lights strung over the high street that draws our eyes as the mignon gold- and silver-wrapped choccies, shimmering sugared almonds, marzipan figurines of snowmen and Santa, and striped candy canes and lollies. And we intend to have all of these.

Homemade truffles come top of my list if I'm going to get melting. These couldn't be easier, especially when they are square as opposed to round, and don't call for rolling. Add a drop of your favourite hooch – pretty much anything goes with chocolate, so design them with the receiver in mind. Brandy and rum are ever Christmassy, but more normally I surreptitiously spirit a few tablespoons of whatever fine whisky or Calvados my husband's got in. And unlike so many bought truffles, here you can guarantee a really good high percentage cocoa chocolate.

The modern fad of chocolate slabs is also welcome. These couldn't be prettier or easier, and can be themed in any number of festive ways, with dried cranberries and sour cherries, slivers of candied peel, walnuts and toasted hazelnuts, Brazil nuts, glacé cherries, or with a Christmas tree traced in Smarties, a snowman or a stocking.

Homemade chocolates make great presents, as do jars of chutneys and herb jellies. They're bound to be appreciated with all those impromptu lunches of the end of the roast with some salads, that are given a second life with a lovely relish of some sort. Even more luxurious is a clementine curd spiked with Cointreau, so deliciously decadent on Boxing Day morning with some toasted brioche or warm croissants.

My granny had a fondness for chocolate violets, ginger wine and liquid-filled jellies, so these take me back. And they're very pretty, though be sure to use a low-percentage cocoa dark chocolate rather than a high one, which will bloom.

violet medallions

100g dark chocolate (approx.
  50% cocoa), broken into pieces
25g white chocolate, e.g. Green
  & Black's, broken into pieces
crystallised violets

Makes approx. 25

Gently melt the two chocolates separately in bowls set over pans with a little simmering water in them. At the same time, tear off a large sheet of baking paper, and draw circles about 4cm in diameter on it (I use a tealight as a guide). Turn the paper over on the work surface and spread about half a teaspoon of dark chocolate inside each circle, using the outline to shape it. If the white chocolate has started to set again, gently reheat it. Drop a small dot in the centre of the dark chocolate, and swirl it using a cocktail stick or the tip of a skewer. Place a crystallised violet in the centre. Leave the discs to harden completely in a cool place for an hour or two. Peel the medallions off the paper, and store in an airtight container – they will be good for several days.

The milk chocolate drizzle is gooier than the dark chocolate base, a little like the inside of a truffle, which gives a lovely contrast. And the decoration could be anything graphic that takes your imagination. But the Christmas tree with silvery lights should melt any heart.

polka dot slab

450g dark chocolate
   (approx. 50% cocoa), broken
   into pieces
100g milk chocolate, broken
   into pieces
2 tablespoons strong black coffee
Smarties or white chocolate buttons,
   and silver or coloured balls
   to decorate

Makes 1 x 32 x 23cm slab

Gently melt the dark and milk chocolate in separate bowls over pans with a little simmering water in them. Blend the coffee into the milk chocolate a tablespoon at a time, which will darken it in colour. Line the base of a 32 x 23cm Swiss roll tin with clingfilm. Pour the dark chocolate over the base, smoothing the surface, and drizzle the milk chocolate on top in swirls. Once you are confident the chocolate is completely cool, use Smarties or white buttons to make a Christmas tree standing in a pot in the centre of the slab, and scatter some balls in between the buttons to create the effect of fairy lights. Set aside in a cool place to harden for several hours.

To serve, carefully remove the clingfilm on the base, and place on a board or plate. Cut into it over coffee. It keeps well for several days.

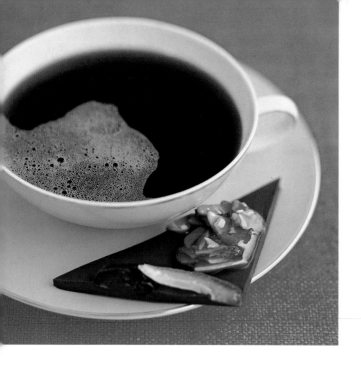

If you have ever tried to make florentines you will know they are much fiddlier and harder to get right than their appearance suggests. This simple slab has all the treasures for which we love them, in particular that toffee almond brittle. At this time of year there are some gorgeous candied peels to take advantage of – try to buy it by the segment and slice it yourself.

florentine slab

50g flaked almonds

400g dark chocolate (approx. 50% cocoa), broken into pieces

100g white caster sugar

50g undyed glacé cherries, halved

30g candied orange peel, cut into thin slivers about 2cm long

Makes 1 x 32 x 23cm slab

Preheat the oven to 180°C fan/200°C/gas mark 6. Spread the almonds out in a thin layer in a shallow baking dish and toast for 8–10 minutes, until lightly golden, then remove from the oven and leave to cool.

Line a 32 x 23cm Swiss roll tin with clingfilm. Gently melt the chocolate in a bowl set over a pan with a little simmering water in it, removing the bowl now and again and stirring to avoid overheating. Smooth the melted chocolate over the base of the tin.

At the same time place the sugar and 50ml water in a small saucepan, bring to the boil and simmer over a low heat for about 15 minutes until a deep gold, swirling it occasionally as it starts to colour to ensure it caramelises evenly. Stir in the nuts. Scatter clusters over the surface of the chocolate, then scatter over the cherries and candied peel. Set aside in a cool place for several hours to set. The slab should keep for a couple of days; it will still taste good beyond this, but may develop a bloom. Set aside, and avoid covering as trapped moisture will again cause the chocolate to bloom.

There are some beautiful nougats on the market, ones with dried raspberries and blueberries in them and the like.

nougat cups

100ml double cream
100g dark chocolate (approx. 70% cocoa), broken into pieces
½ teaspoon vanilla extract
150g nougat, cut into small nibs
silver or gold balls, or chocolate shavings to decorate (optional)

Makes approx. 20

Arrange about twenty paper petits fours cases on a small tray or in a roasting dish. Bring the cream to the boil in a small non-stick saucepan. Pour it over the chocolate in a bowl, leave for a minute or two and then give it a stir, and repeat this until the chocolate has completely melted and you have a thick cream. Stir in the vanilla, then fold in the nougat nibs.

Fill the paper cases with the mixture – if you like you can scatter over a few silver or gold balls, or chocolate shavings. Loosely cover with clingfilm and chill for a few hours. These should keep well for about a week in the fridge.

If you're married to a whisky lover, as I am, you're unlikely to get much of a pop at that fine bottle of single malt that comes his way over Christmas. I insist on being left my angel's share or the near equivalent, a wee nip for some chocolate truffles. The last such fine bottle was a seventeen-year-old Highland single malt whisky from the Adelphi distillery, which specialises in rare whiskies.

These truffles take the easy way out – we can't be doing with all that rolling and dipping demanded by round ones. With this method, for the sake of some ten minutes' labour you end up with a large bowl of meltingly creamy square truffles.

whisky galore truffles

400ml double cream
400g dark chocolate (approx.
    70% cocoa), broken into pieces
2 tablespoons whisky, ideally
    single malt
approx. 25g cocoa

Makes 800g

Bring the cream to the boil in a small non-stick saucepan. Pour it over the chocolate in a bowl, leave for a minute or two and then give it a stir, then repeat this until the chocolate has completely melted and you have a thick cream. Stir in the whisky.

Next you want a square or oblong baking dish in which to set a slab just under 2cm in depth. I use a 23cm square brownie tin, and end up with a rectangle about 15 x 23cm. First line the tin with clingfilm, with plenty overhanging the sides, enough to fold one end back over the top of the slab once you pour it. Pour the chocolate into one end of the tin, allowing it to spread towards the other, and fold the clingfilm at this end back over the slab, so you have a rectangle about 15 x 23 x 2cm, smoothing the surface with your fingers. Tuck the clingfilm ends underneath the tin to keep the slab in place and chill for several hours until set.

Sift the cocoa into a large bowl, and turn the slab out on to a work surface. Trim the edges and cut into 1.5cm cubes. Place about a third of these in the bowl, and swirl to coat them in cocoa. Remove them with your hands, giving them a little shake in your palm to dust off any excess cocoa, then pile into a large bowl, or bowls, and repeat with the remainder. Cover and chill until required, removing them from the fridge about 30 minutes before eating. They will keep for several days – you can always dust them with a little more cocoa if it seems to have been absorbed.

The perfect chutney to serve with leftover duck and goose, and equally good with turkey and the cheeseboard. You can dip in as soon as it's made, or let it mature for a few months. Clip-top Le Parfait jars are ideal, and like most chutneys this is a good keeper.

fig, star anise and port chutney

750g ready-to-eat dried figs, stalks trimmed, sliced

500g eating apples, quartered, cored and diced

700g red onions, peeled, halved and sliced

3 star anise

6 green cardamom pods

1 x 7cm cinnamon stick

500ml red wine vinegar

400ml apple juice

450g soft brown sugar

1 tablespoon sea salt

150ml port

Makes approx. 1.5 litres

Place the figs, apples and onions in a large saucepan. Add the spices, wrapping the star anise and cardamom in a small square of muslin or cotton, for ease of removing them at the end. Pour over the vinegar. Add the apple juice, sugar and salt and stir, then bring to a simmer and cook over a low heat for 3–3½ hours, adding the port about an hour before the end of cooking. Stir occasionally, but more frequently towards the end to prevent the chutney from sticking.

It's difficult to specify exactly how long the chutney will take to cook, as this will depend on the size of your pan and the heat at which you simmer it. Don't worry about paying too much attention at the beginning, but keep a watchful eye towards the end. There should still be a small amount of sticky syrup floating on the surface, bearing in mind the chutney will firm up on cooling. To test it, spread a couple of tablespoons on a cold plate, leave it to cool for a few minutes, then judge whether it is the right consistency. Once the chutney is cooked, discard the spices.

Heat three 0.5 litre clip-top jars (or whatever jars you are using) for 5 minutes in a medium hot oven (about 170°C fan/190°C/gas mark 3). Fill the hot jars with the hot chutney, then close them and leave to cool.

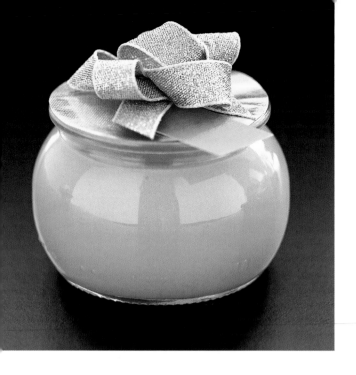

There is something slightly risqué about this curd, which makes it so apt for spreading on toast for breakfast or tea during the festive season. You can also use it to fill little pastry cases for pud. As curd has a limited shelf life, this should do for several friends, divided between small pots or jars.

clementine curd with cointreau

juice of 2 clementines
finely grated zest and juice
    of ½ lemon
2 tablespoons Cointreau
6 medium organic eggs
180g unsalted butter, diced
270g golden caster sugar

Makes 600–700ml

Heat all the ingredients in a small non-stick saucepan over a low heat, whisking constantly until the butter melts. Continue to stir with a wooden spoon until it thickens into a custard. While this takes time, it happens very quickly at the end, so it's worth being patient. Care must be taken that it doesn't boil, otherwise it will curdle, but don't worry if it seems slightly lumpy.

Pass the curd through a sieve into a bowl, then divide between jars or small bowls. Cover, and chill once cool, when it will set. It will keep well for at least a couple of weeks if stored in the fridge.

A colourful and chunky piccalilli that can be eaten as soon as it is made.
Sprinkle it with chopped coriander and serve it like a little salad aside.

chunky piccalilli

2 tablespoons extra virgin olive oil

1 red pepper, core and seeds removed,
   cut into 1cm strips

200g cauliflower florets, stalks trimmed

150g romesco florets

4 fresh medium-hot red chillies, left whole

2 medium carrots, ends removed, peeled
   and cut into 8 batons each

6 shallots, peeled

2 tablespoons cider
   or white wine vinegar

500ml white wine

100ml water

2 teaspoons ground ginger

1 teaspoon turmeric

2 teaspoons golden caster sugar

1 bay leaf

1½ teaspoons sea salt

2 teaspoons cornflour, blended
   with 1 tablespoon water

2 teaspoons wholegrain mustard

Makes approx. 1.2 litres

Heat the olive oil in a large saucepan over a medium heat. Add all the vegetables and fry for a few minutes, stirring occasionally. Add the vinegar, wine and water, the spices, sugar, bay leaf and salt, then bring to the boil and simmer over a low heat for 20 minutes, stirring occasionally. Stir in the cornflour paste and simmer for a couple of minutes longer until the sauce thickens. Stir in the mustard, transfer to a bowl and leave to cool.

If you are planning on eating the pickle within a few hours, cover and set aside somewhere cool. If you are keeping it for a few days, chill and bring it back up to room temperature before serving. If, however, you are making it for a present or want to bottle it, first sterilise your jars. Wash and dry them, then place them in an oven preheated to 170°C fan/190°C/gas mark 3, for 5 minutes. Remove and fill with the hot vegetables, packing them down, then pour over the liquor. Seal the jars with their lids and leave to cool completely. Store in the fridge for up to a month.

Shimmering herb jellies make a lovely present over Christmas, and are almost certain to make a welcome appearance at the table at some point of the festivities, with some cold meat.

herb jelly

1.5kg cooking apples
400ml cider vinegar
50g fresh rosemary sprigs
approx. 750g granulated
　　sugar

Makes
1.2–1.5 litres

Cut the unpeeled, uncored apples into pieces and place in a large saucepan with the vinegar, 800ml of water, and half the rosemary. Bring to the boil, then simmer over a very low heat for 1 hour. Now tip the contents of the pan into a jelly bag suspended over a large bowl – I find it easiest to fill the bag in the bowl before lifting it up. Leave to drip through for at least a couple of hours, or overnight. You should end up with a cloudy pink juice. Don't actually squeeze the bag or you will jeopardise the next stage, when the juice clarifies.

Place a few little dishes or saucers in the freezer. Measure the juice into a large saucepan – you should have about 900ml. Add 500g of sugar for every 600ml of juice. Bring to the boil, stirring occasionally until the sugar melts, and simmer for 15 minutes. Meanwhile, preheat the oven to 170°C fan/190°C/gas mark 3, and sterilise your open jars for 5 minutes. These should be warm when you fill them. Skim the rubbery white scum off the jelly. To test whether it is ready, spoon a little into one of the chilled dishes and place in the freezer for a few minutes. If it appears thickened, and a skin has formed that wrinkles when you drag your finger through it, it is ready. Otherwise simmer it for another 5 minutes and try again.

Pop a few rosemary sprigs into each warm jar and fill them with the jelly. Cover with a clean tea towel and leave to cool for a couple of hours or until the jelly has begun to set, then press the herbs down to suspend them. Re-cover the jelly and leave to cool to room temperature, then seal and leave overnight. The jelly should keep well, stored in a cool environment, for several months.

*A hooped jelly bag is a muslin sack sewn on to a wooden hoop. It can be hooked over a cupboard doorknob above the work surface, or from a slatted shelf, with the bowl beneath. In the absence of a hooped jelly bag, it is easy enough to make your own. Open out a wire coat hanger into a circle and pin a clean tea-towel over the rim to form a bag. Now tie two long string handles in place at right angles to each other, to hang it up.

index

acknowledgements

With many thanks to Angela Mason, to my agent Rosemary Sandberg, to Suzanna de Jong, Editor, Annie Lee, Copy Editor, and to
Kyle Cathie. And with love and thanks to Jonnie, Rothko and Louis.